PRAYER IS SIMPLY TALKING TO GOD

It's Not Complicated. Just Talk to God

PAULINE ADONGO

WESTBOW
PRESS®
A DIVISION OF THOMAS NELSON
& ZONDERVAN

Scripture quotations marked (NIV) are taken from the Holy Bible, New International Version®, NIV®. Copyright © 1973, 1978, 1984, 2011 by Biblica, Inc.™ Used by permission of Zondervan. All rights reserved worldwide. www.zondervan.com The "NIV" and "New International Version" are trademarks registered in the United States Patent and Trademark Office by Biblica, Inc.™

Scripture taken from the New King James Version®. Copyright © 1982 by Thomas Nelson. Used by permission. All rights reserved.

Scripture quotations are taken from the Holy Bible, New Living Translation, copyright ©1996, 2004, 2007, 2013, 2015 by Tyndale House Foundation. Used by permission of Tyndale House Publishers, Inc., Carol Stream, Illinois 60188. All rights reserved.

Cover Photo by DLWV Creative, Media, PA ; Makeup by Tutu_artistry Instagram, Philadelphia, PA

WestBow Press books may be ordered through booksellers or by contacting:

WestBow Press
A Division of Thomas Nelson & Zondervan
1663 Liberty Drive
Bloomington, IN 47403
www.westbowpress.com
1 (866) 928-1240

Because of the dynamic nature of the Internet, any web addresses or links contained in this book may have changed since publication and may no longer be valid. The views expressed in this work are solely those of the author and do not necessarily reflect the views of the publisher, and the publisher hereby disclaims any responsibility for them.

Any people depicted in stock imagery provided by Thinkstock are models, and such images are being used for illustrative purposes only. Certain stock imagery © Thinkstock.

ISBN: 978-1-5127-6698-1 (sc)
ISBN: 978-1-5127-6699-8 (e)

Library of Congress Control Number: 2016920115

Print information available on the last page.

WestBow Press rev. date: 12/19/2016

DEDICATION

I am dedicating this book to my nieces: Madison,
Haile, and Deedee. God is a respecter of no one.
He sees all of us equally. Make a habit of talking
to God frequently. He always hears us when
we talk to Him or rather when we pray.

Love, Polly

FORWARD

Pauline's book on prayer is a blessing! Many people make prayer more complicated than it is. As Pauline points out, it is communicating with our Father. When we look at it with eyes like this, childlike in faith, our hope rises. We have a good Father! Pauline has a rich testimony and an intimacy with the Lord that truly inspires others. Prayer is communicating with our creator, the lover of our soul, the one who knows us and our lives better than we know ourselves. The one who has awesome plans for us, who has happy thoughts towards us, and as Pauline notes, has made us perfect in His Son. As we Listen to the Lord, talk to him, praise Him, we grow in intimacy with the One who made and loves us. Pauline is a gifted woman of God! I recommend her book to anyone who loves the Lord.

Jennifer Matty
Director of Ministry Teams
East Gate Church, West Chester, Pennsylvania, USA

CONTENTS

†

CONTENTS

PREFACE

†

In the summer of 2015 I more actively started venturing into the ministerial journey, and it has been very exciting and insightful. On the subject of prayer, my observations so far are that most believers, both young and old, have a misconstrued notion about prayer. Some think that prayer should be left only to those assigned as intercessors or pastors, ministers, elders and deacons. Surprisingly, a good number of those called in these positions are not comfortable with prayer either!

One of my character traits is that I am too observant. I have also been around married couples who when asked to pray will gesture to the other, asking their spouses to pray instead. Some even comment, *"Oh, my wife prays better" or "My wife is the prayer warrior."* The wife may in turn respond, *"No, you are the pastor or elder, you should pray!"* Generally, and this is strictly based on observations, males will be quiet and ladies will volunteer to pray. Often, there is overwhelming hesitation to pray, but be encouraged! Each of us, any one of us, can pray.

Some believers have convinced themselves that they do not know how to pray. I once asked a lady to pray at the end of training session and she responded adamantly, *"No Pauline, I cannot shout loud enough."* I was grieved internally by that response. I recall my heart just sinking into a deep whimper. I was saddened that this sister equated prayer to shouting and that she thought her prayers were not good enough. It is from this experience, and also with the leading of the Holy Spirit, that I was inspired to write this book. My heart ached; I really wanted to help believers attain confidence and become comfortable with praying. I sought to demystify misconceptions, false beliefs, and religious practices associated to prayer. These areas are all discussed in this book.

We are living in times where prayer is essential and paramount to each believer. In these times, prayer is a necessity, and each believer should be confident in knowing that their prayers, regardless of how they are presented to God, are heard. This understanding also delivers the believer from co-dependence on spiritual leaders such as pastors, those called in the five-fold ministry, and even their prayer partners as their sole source of prayer. Whereas some have the gift of intercession or intercessory prayer, each believer can pray. The purpose of writing this book is to help those struggling with praying, to understand what prayer means, and to get comfortable with this subject and attain freedom, courage, and confidence to pray independently.

CONCEPTS OF PRAYER

†

It would be best to start with defining prayer. Prayer is simply communicating to God. Prayer is among the various forms of communication we use to talk to God. We also use singing, clapping, dancing, and art as ways to communicate with Him. At creation, God intended for us to have fellowship with Him. We were created to worship, honor, and adore God; read Psalms 150; and the bulk of these are done through prayer. Like any healthy human relationship, God desires that we maintain contact with Him, and one of the ways we do this is through prayer. Prayer is talking to God.

You may ask then, what do we talk to God about? The shorter answer to this question is that we talk or should talk to God about anything and everything. I will elaborate on what to talk about in the upcoming chapters, but consider this for now: Since we have been reconciled to God through Jesus Christ, we have been adopted as sons and daughters. This makes God our Father, which in turn makes it possible now to talk directly to God about any area of our lives.

There is more that God wants to share and inform us of in this wonderful relationship. It's a one of kind relationship where God really wants to show us some deep, secretive treasures towards the destiny He has for us. In Jeremiah 33.3, God says, *"Call to Me, and I will answer you, and show you great and mighty things, which you do not need."*(NKJV). So we talk to God about these great and mighty things, these mysteries that He wants to reveal or has already revealed to us. Prayer starts this conversation going.

When we talk to God, He also speaks back to us just as it would happen in regular communication with a human being. There are various ways in which God responds to us in prayer. The mode of response varies from person to person but God responds back. God talks or responds to us using the mode a person would best understand or hear. Given that God is our creator, He knows us inside and out. He will communicate back to us in the form that He knows we will grasp. To some, God communicates through an audible voice, and to others through an inner voice, music, Scriptures, an inner knowing, dreams, visions, angelic visitations, physical and auditory senses, smells and even colors. Overall, you need to know that He talks back to us.

Consider this as you read along to the next chapter: It is through prayer that the inner things of God are revealed and God's power through the Holy Spirit is manifested. The gifts of the Holy Spirit are also imparted through prayer, and it is through prayer that we fight spiritual warfare to bring down strongholds and satanic dominions. However, through prayer we also assert our authority and war from a position of victory as we declare God's Kingdom, promises, and blessings over us. It is through prayer that we receive revelation and clarity concerning the plans God has for us. It is also through prayer that new dreams are birthed, destinies are activated, and new ideas and creativity occur by the Holy Spirit. By prayer we are strengthened, healed, delivered, protected, and saved. Prayer is the foundation to a fulfilled Christian life. The exceeding, abundance, and overflow all stem from prayer.

ASPECTS OF PRAYER

†

Shortly after I gave my life to Christ in 1983, I was taught by pastor, now Archbishop, Jonah Bedan of Christian Outreach Ministries based in Nakuru Kenya, East Africa. He taught me the following aspects of prayer. These have stuck with me since then. These prayer aspects mirror the prayer that Jesus taught His disciples, commonly known as the Lord's Prayer from Luke 11:1-4:

> *One day Jesus was praying in a certain place. When he finished, one of his disciples said to him, "Lord, teach us to pray, just as John taught his disciples." He said to them, "When you pray, say: Father, hallowed be your name, your kingdom come. Thy will be done on earth as it is in heaven. Give us each day our daily bread. Forgive us our sins, for we also forgive everyone who sins against us. And lead us not into temptation. For thine is thy kingdom, and the power and the glory forever." (NKJ)*

The Lord's Prayer is frequently recited and prayed in many fellowships. So let us start this chapter by reviewing the key aspects of the Lord's Prayer and how we can apply them in our prayers.

Our Father—The reason we address God as our Father is because He created us. We were created in the image of God (Genesis 1:26, *"Let us create man in our own image"* (NKJV). We stem from God by this virtue. Though sin later came to the earth through Adam, we are later reconciled through Christ by His love dying for us to make us sons and daughters. *"Behold what manner of love the Father has bestowed on us, that we should be called children of God"* (1 John 3:1, NKJV). Christ's sacrifice gives us the adoption, and now as children we have Father.

In prayer, therefore, we approach God as our Father. Not as a strange unreachable person, but as someone we relate to closely as a child would relate to a Father. As mentioned in the preface, God desires for fellowship, so in prayer, we approach Him freely as a Father that is open for fellowship and conversation.

I would like to clear up a misconception here as well. Many think we pray to Jesus directly. However, this should not be. Jesus Himself prayed to God His Father who is also our Father. So we too pray to our Father, not to Jesus. As believers, we now pray directly to God, by the Holy Spirit, in the name of Jesus, and appropriating the Blood that was shed and the Word of God, which is our testimony.

The Only One God—Believers and Christians only pray and should pray to one God, Jehovah. This is the first commandment as stated in Exodus 20:2-6:

> *I am the Lord your God, who brought you out of the land of Egypt, out of the house of bondage. You shall have no other gods before Me. You shall not make for yourself a carved image any likeness of anything that is in heaven above, or that is in the earth beneath, or that is in the water under the earth; you shall not bow down to them nor serve them. For I, the Lord your God, am a jealous God, visiting the iniquity of the fathers upon the children to the third and fourth generations of those who hate Me, but showing mercy to thousands, to those who love Me and keep My commandments. (NKJV)*

In prayer, we pray to only one God in obedience to His commandments that we shall worship no other god but Him. We do not pray to multiple gods or deities or images or anything God created such as the moon, stars, or sun, or any other terrestrial beings. I caution on the inclusion of worldly ideas where believers are taught to call on their stars, suns, dead saints, or family in prayer.

I once visited a fellowship whose prayer leader that night kept instructing the members to *"Call on your sun, call on your stars."* Right there I shut my mouth and started to pray fervently in my prayer language. All the while I was thinking, "Why is this woman instructing to call on the sun and stars?" On this particular night, God opened my eyes and understanding to recognize false spirits that camouflage during prayer or worship. I strongly advise against such prayers as they not only unscriptural, but they also open doors to the demonic, occult practices as well as necromancy. The Bible warns that such practices are false as they exchange the truth about God for lies; worshiping and serving the creation instead of the Creator; our God! For more information, read Romans 1:24-25.

God instructs and cautions against calling any mediums or the dead. I also advise against murmuring or repeating statements you are clueless about as you really don't know who or what you may be praying to. Such statements are common in yoga practices or meditation type classes. If is not the real scripture acknowledging the Trinity and Jesus as the resurrected Lord and Savior, do not say it! Here are some scriptures you can reference:

♦ **Deuteronomy 18:9-13**: *-When you enter the land the LORD your God is giving you, do not learn to imitate the detestable ways of the nations there. Let no one be found among you who sacrifices his son or daughter in the fire, who practices divination or sorcery, interprets omens, engages in witchcraft, or casts spells, or who is a medium or spiritist or who consults the dead. Anyone who does these things is detestable to the LORD, and because of these detestable practices the LORD your God will drive out those nations before you. You must be blameless before the LORD your God. (NKJV)*

♦ **Leviticus: 19:31-***Do not turn to mediums or seek out spiritists, for you will be defiled by them. I am the LORD your God. (NIV)*

◆ **Leviticus 20:6:**-*I will set my face against the person who turns to mediums and spiritists to prostitute himself by following them, and I will cut him off from his people. (NKJV)*

We pray to God as the ultimate Supreme God and the Creator of everything. We pray to God who is called Jehovah. We pray to God our Father.

Worship or Adoration—Just as you would first acknowledge anyone of honor by his or her title, we too must first approach God in reverence of Him. Our prayers should start by worshipping and honoring God. We do this by acknowledging His Lordship over us and His sovereignty as the Supreme God.

As demonstrated in the Lord's Prayer, this acknowledgement is shown by the phrase "*hallowed by thy Name, thy kingdom come.*" By first worshiping God, we declare His Majesty and sovereignty. A sample prayer of worship or adoration is: "*God our Father we bless your name, we adore you alone are God, we worship you, we declare that you are only God, most high, exalted, worthy, majesty, omnipotent, holy.*"

Worship is an ultimate form of prayer because in worship it is always all about God not us. Worship is a true sacrifice of ourselves where the flesh dies, and our needs and wants are set aside. All that is left is attention and focus God. When we say or sing "we bring sacrifice of praise into the house of the Lord and offer the sacrifice of thanksgiving," we are worshipping, letting go, and focusing on God.

In the book of Revelation, you see the twenty-four elders bowing down repeatedly, worshiping God. Revelation 4:10-11:

> *The twenty-four elders fall down before him who sits on the throne and worship him who lives forever and ever. They lay their crowns before the throne and say: "You are worthy, our Lord and God, to receive glory and honor*

and power, for you created all things and by your will
they were created and have their being." (NKJV)

Worship is what we will do when we go to heaven, so why not practice more of it here on earth?

Repeatedly throughout the Bible, whenever God spoke to prophets or sent messengers, every encounter was first met with worship because the recipients of the message saw or sensed God's presence. Worship always preceded the message and was often done after an encounter with God. For example, Mary worshiped God after she heard from the angel about conceiving Jesus. Moses worshipped the Lord before his encounter with the burning bush. Abraham, Moses, and Jacob built various altars following encounters with God.

I encourage you to spend more time in worshiping God while praying. Put aside the needs and wants for a while and just stay focused in worshiping God. You can play worship music, sing, and verbally utter these words to God: *"Lord I bless You, You are holy, honor and glory be unto You."* Keep worshipping before you transition to other aspects of prayer.

Your Kingdom Come and Your will be done on earth as it is in Heaven—It is quite revealing that Jesus decrees God's Kingdom at the beginning of the prayer. This serves as a reminder that as believers we pray from a position of victory. Praying from a victorious position is very effective and strategic in all areas of prayers, but more importantly, in spiritual warfare.

The will of God is God's Kingdom, and whatever happens in heaven happens on earth for us. Health, longevity, peace, abundance, wholeness, joy, and fullness of life are all in heaven. So, when we pray from victory we counter the negative with what is already in heaven; we degree God's promises and thoughts on us!

In the Lord's Prayer, we notice that the phrase "thy will be done on earth as it is in heaven" is stated before "give us this day our daily bread." This represents our attitude as we approach prayer. It is important that we pray the will of God for our lives and not just our fleshly desires in order to get our prayers answered. James warns that we pray amiss because we leave God's will out and only ask out of our own desires. So, for any issue that we present to God in prayer, we should evaluate the will of God concerning the issue. This is done by utilizing the Bible to research the specific areas that we want to petition God for.

Forgive us our sins as we forgive those who sin against us—This is the repentance or confession aspect of prayer. More and more I find it easier to approach prayer more boldly after repenting. With the help of the Holy Spirit, I am learning to be quick to forgive. At times this has been difficult because some offenses or situations really hit hard. In such times I call more on the Holy Spirit and ask for His help. I simply say *"Holy Spirit help me forgive this person and take it out of my system."*

Most of the time, the same Holy Spirit also helps me reevaluate myself and examine what my role was in that offense. When I am wrong, I frequently ask the person I offended to forgive me. From studying "forgiveness," I have learned that it is good to state the actual offense while asking for forgiveness. For example, instead of saying *"forgive me for offending you,"* I would be more specific and say: *"Mom, forgive me. I was harsh when I responded to you last night. Will you please forgive me?"* I have actually said this to my Mom.

Repentance also means turning back from the wrong that I did. Actually, I have heard repentance as turning the opposite direction of the wrong you did and not revisiting the issue. So, in the example I gave above, if I asked my Mom to forgive my offense but I keep being harsh to her, then I really did not repent. On the other hand, if my Mom keeps reminding me of the offense, shares my offense to other people, or keeps bringing it up, then she really has not forgiven me.

I also believe in genuine, intentional, and timely repentance By this I do not mean one has to be convicted deeply in order to repent, but you must be sincere first to yourself, to God, and then to the person you offended. A bad example of repentance is asking for forgiveness knowing very well you are going to go back to what you've just repented for. Another bad example is repentance as a religious activity to show remorse without actually meaning it. Sadly, repentance tends to be a scarcity in this day and age. Some believe that once saved, all is well, and they can live a compromised life and just approach God anyhow. This is not to say we should be sin-conscious but we should walk in the fear for *"God is Spirit and those who serve Him must also serve Him in truth and righteousness* (John 4:24 NKJV). Be sincere in your repentance. Mean it, own it, do it, leave it, and move on!

I shared earlier in this section that I am learning to be quick to repent or ask forgiveness from the person I offended. This continues to be a work in process, but I strongly advise that you really seek the help of the Holy Spirit on "timeliness." The reason for this is because at times the offense may still be very fresh, and it may hurt deeply to approach the perpetrator. The most challenging part from personal experience is approaching the person you need to repent to when the person ignores or refuses to accept your apology. Tougher yet is asking for forgiveness from a person when you absolutely know that there was no wrong done on your part. Oh do I call on the Holy Spirit at such times!

This is what the Holy Spirit has led me to do: First is to reflect on the scriptures, "forgive and you shall be forgiven" (Matthew 6:14, NKJV) and to "confess your sins to one another that you may be healed" (James 5:16, NKJV). **Next** is to look at the person through the eyes of love, Christ's love. What does Christ teach under such circumstances? I reflect on Christ's teachings and other scriptures such as:

- **Matthew 6:14-15**: *"For if you forgive men when they sin against you, your heavenly Father will also forgive you. But if you do not forgive men their sins, your Father will not forgive your sins."* *(NKJV)*

- **Matthew 18:21-22**: *"Then Peter came to Him and said, 'Lord, how often shall my brother sin against me, and I forgive him? Up to seven times'(NKJV)*. Here Jesus Christ teaches His disciples to forgive countlessly, so I must do the same.

- **Proverbs 25:21-22**:*" If thine enemy be hungry, give him bread to eat; and if he be thirsty, give him water to drink: For thou shalt heap coals of fire upon his head, and the Lord shall reward you."* *(NKJV)*

I also enjoy 1 Corinthians 13:1-13 as this chapter highlights love as the foundation for everything. I reference these Scriptures more frequently to help me with how to deal with people on a daily basis and whenever I have to react to offenses. We forgive because Christ loved us so much to die for us, and now that we are saved, we too should extend that love to others. Allow agape love to help you forgive quickly, forgive the unforgivable, and even to forgive when you have done no wrong.

The following is sample prayer of repentance:

> *Father I come to you through the blood of Jesus. I repent of all my sins. I confess any sin of the mind, soul mouth, of action or thought, against you, the Holy Spirit or my siblings, friends or family, husband or person. I release any bitterness or anger. I forgive whoever offended me. I receive your forgiveness by the blood. I turn away from my sins, I thank you for forgiving and forgetting my sins. In Jesus name. Amen*

In the next chapter, I outline some advantages of repentance.

ADVANTAGES OF REPENTANCE
AND FORGIVENESS

†

As I shared in the previous chapter, forgiveness brings such peace and freedom to proceed with praying. In addition to these, there are other advantages to repenting and asking others to forgive our offenses. Here are some advantages of confessing our sins:

♦ God forgives and never remembers our sins. *"When we confess our sins, God is faithful and just to forgive our sins and cleanse us from all our righteousness"* (1 John 1:9. NKJV). In addition to being forgiven, God assures us that He does not remember any of our sins. This assurance is in Hebrews 8:12: *"For I will be merciful to their unrighteousness, and their sins and their iniquities will I remember no more."* (NKJV)

♦ God hears our prayers and heals us when we repent. Confession or repentance of our sin removes any barriers and clears the air of anything that would cause God not to hear our prayers. God in turn responds with answers. *"If my people, which are called by my name, shall humble themselves, and pray, and seek my face, and turn from their wicked ways; then will I hear from heaven, and will forgive their sin, and will heal their land"* (2 Chronicles 7:14, NKJV).

♦ We attain boldness and confidence to approach God in prayer. Since God hears and forgives us once we repent, we are now free to approach God. The Blood of Jesus blots out sins to reconcile with God our Father. This allows us to come to God our Father with more boldly. Hebrews 4:16 explains this: *"We have a great High Priest who has passed through the heavens, Jesus the Son of God, let us hold fast our confession. For we do not have a High Priest who cannot sympathize with our weaknesses, but was in all points tempted as we are, yet without sin. Let us therefore come boldly to the throne of grace that we may obtain mercy and find grace to help in time of need." (NKJV)*

● Repentance makes us free from shame and guilt. There is no more condemnation after true repentance. After repenting we should be careful not to allow Satan to remind our sins or make us feel guilty. Anyone or anything that condemns you is not of God. God is merciful and loving. Any thought of past sin is purposed by Satan to bring us guilt. So, we must denounce Satan by quoting the verses: *"There is no condemnation to those who are in Christ Jesus"* (Romans 8:1-2, NKJV) and *"As far as the east if from the west, God does not remember my sins"* (Hebrews 10: 17-18, NJVK).

● Repentance brings us refreshment. You may experience this already. Usually after asking for forgiveness and reconciling it feels like a heavy burden has been lifted off one's shoulders. You may experience some lightness as well. After this, there normally develops close connections or improved relationships, as well as an increase in ideas and creativity. One may even experience a fresh start of looking at things from a new perspective. Such are examples of refreshments from God. In Acts 3:19, we are instructed to: *"Repent, then, and turn to God, so that your sins may be wiped out, that times of refreshing may come from the Lord . . ." (NIV)*

ASPECTS OF PRAYER—CONTINUED

We are still reviewing aspects of prayer based on the Lord's Prayer in in this chapter. I will discuss the remainder of the Lord's Prayer and its applicability in daily prayer. First, the prayer itself: *"Our Father, hallowed be your name, your kingdom come. Thy will be done on earth as it is in heaven. Give us each day our daily bread. Forgive us our sins, for we also forgive everyone who sins against us. And lead us not into temptation. For thine is thy kingdom, and the power and the glory forever".* (NKJV) Let us review the remainder of the prayers below:

Asking for Our Needs—You may have noticed that asking God for our needs comes much later in prayer and is not something that is done immediately when we start praying. If we would compare this to normal human relations, it could be wrong not to acknowledge a person, and instead just approach me initially with a request.

In this stage of prayer, which is also referred as "petitioning" or supplications, we make our needs known to God just as it in the Lord's Prayer, *"give us this day our daily bread."* Petitioning is making a request with respect to a particular course. In this stage of prayer, we ask God for what we want. We do this in confidence and courage, approaching God as our Father.

The following are ways we can go about petitioning:

Ask God for what you want. There are limitations on what you can ask God. The promise to ask God for our needs supported by the scriptures in Luke 11:9-10. This scripture reads, *"So I say to we, ask, and it will be given to we; seek, and we will find; knock, and it will be opened to we. For everyone who asks receives, and he who seeks finds, and to him who knocks it will be opened."* (NKJV)

Ask according to God's will. God's will is what He created us for. We find these in His promises and plans for us. When we petition, we ask God for what we want according to His will. God will grant us what when need if it lines us with His Will we can also ask God for anything according to 1 John 5:14, which is a good scripture to reference when praying according to God's will. *"This is the confidence we have in approaching God: that if we ask anything according to his will, He hears us." (NKJV)*

Asking without anxiety or fear. As God's children we can approach God courageously knowing that we have been forgiven and without fear of retribution or judgment. God, according to Philippians 4:6, asks us to *"Be anxious for nothing, but in everything by prayer and supplication with thanksgiving let your requests be made known to God." (NKJV)*

We petition God with the assurance that He is the Creator of all things. God knows our desires and He is able to supply us what we need according to Philippians 4:19: *"God shall supply all your need according to His riches in glory by Christ Jesus." (NKJV)*

We ask by faith, believing that God hears us, and He will answer our prayers according to James 1:6-8. We must believe in the God that we are praying to that He will answer our request. *"But when we ask, we must believe and not doubt, because the one who doubts is like a wave of the sea, blown and tossed by the wind. That person should not expect to receive anything from the Lord. Such a person is double-minded and unstable in all they do." (NKJV)*

Thanksgiving, Praise, and Worship

In regular conversations it is common to end the interaction by saying thanks to one another. Similarly, we should conclude our prayers by thanking God. Personally, I normally thank God from scriptures or promises related to requests that I petitioned well for. Doing this shifts the focus from the problem to God's promises.

Thanksgiving or praise are acts of faith. At this step in prayer, we believe that God has heard our prayers and has already responded to our requests, so we thank God in advance! In reality this is not different than daily life. Generally, we tend to thank people before they accomplish what we asked them to do. For example, you may ask, "Jonny could you pass me the pen? Thank you." After Jonny brings you then pen, you would thank him again. It is the same concept. We trusted Jonny to bring us the pen when we asked him, so we thanked him. After delivering the pen, we thanked him again. Likewise, we thank God in advance for the answer.

As we conclude the prayer, thanksgiving may lead to praise, singing, dancing, and again reverencing God in worship. So do not be surprised if you transcend into praise and worship at the end of the prayer. Here is an example: *"Lord, I thank you for healing my body. I thank you that I am whole and everything in me including my mind, soul, body is healed. I thank you that I have full recovery. I thank you for supplying every need. I thank you for overflow and abundance. I adore you because you are omnipotent, and nothing shall you withhold from your children. I thank you that you have chosen me as your child and you have prospered me. I bless you Lord. I worship you. In Jesus Name, Amen!"*

The most crucial prayer that is effective involves a) praying in accordance to the will of God and b) praying in faith. Effective prayer is not in the language we use or the sounds and gestures that we make. It is the prayer of faith that brings results. This means then that you can pray or talk to God wherever you are and in the language you are comfortable with.

When we pray to God, we pray through the name of Jesus Christ His son because it is only through Jesus that we can access God. We pray to God through the Son, Jesus Christ, and by the help of the Holy Spirit.

COMMON MISCONCEPTIONS ABOUT PRAYER

†

In this chapter, I would like to highlight some misconceptions about prayer with the hope of bringing clarity and helping those challenged with praying to gain confidence and pursue praying on a regular basis. Here I will address general prayer not intercessory prayer. Common misconceptions include:

Only believers, churchgoers, pastors, and church leaders can pray. This is not true. Anyone can pray because we have established that prayer is simply communicating or talking to God. Praying has no statute, age expectation or limit, or experience or expertise requirement. However, there are those anointed as "intercessors." Intercessors have the gift to pray, and this is their ministry. Besides intercessors, any believer can pray.

You are not good at praying like so and so, and "they pray better than I do." Each of us is uniquely created and specifically anointed by God. You should never compare yourself with anyone else in any area of your life, and the same goes for prayer. Each of us should pray uniquely with the help of the Holy Spirit. So pray in the best way you know how, as led by the Spirit of God. Do not copy others or be intimidated by how others pray. Have confidence in praying in the best way you know how to pray because the Holy Spirit, your helper, is with you.

Prayer must be repeated over and over again in order for God to hear us. The scripture that often helps me to avoid repetitious prayers or reciting prayers is Matthew 6:7. From this verse we learn that citing the problem or request several times does not strike God more than it would the first time you mentioned the issue to Him in prayer. Telling God, the history of the problem would also translate to repetitious prayers. I call it "story telling." Before we approach God, He already knows why we are praying. God knows all. He sees the end from the beginning. There is nothing that happens to us that God does not allow or that He is not aware of. So practice hitting the point, targeting the issue, and moving on to the other aspects of prayer. Jesus taught "*And when you pray, do not use vain repetitions as the heathen do. For they think that they will be heard for their many words. Therefore, do not be like them. For your Father knows the things you have need of before you ask Him*" (Matthew 6:7-8 NKJV).

You need to change the tone of your voice and use specific vocabularies or words while praying. God relates to us in the natural state that He created us in. We should not try to be something else by changing our tones, physical postures, and other ritualistic practices that do not draw God's attention as much as shouting "Hey Lord, I need you help getting this car running!" would. I am not refuting reverencing God during prayer, but we should be mindful of works of the flesh in attempts to move God! I believe such behaviors are learned and are religious, denominational, or cultural, but they do not place a dent in prayer. Assuming a different personality such as changing the tone of voice translates to false humility.

Moreover, God calls us to come to Him as we are. Isaiah 1:18 is a good example of this. Given that once saved we can now relate with Him as friends, it is important to remember that friends do not change their tones or postures while talking to or communicating with each other. Good and real friends are very open and are themselves in their relationship with each other. Be real with God. Talk and relate with Him in prayer normally as you would with a friend. Faith moves God! The prayer of faith is what moves God.

If you allow the Holy Spirit to lead and assist you in prayer. He, the Holy Spirit, will adjust your tone of voice and even guide you to which language or vocabulary to use while praying. I encourage you to ask the Holy Spirit to lead your prayer. You may pray interchangeably in understanding or in tongues, also known as the language of the Holy Spirit or the prayer language. On the other side, the Holy Spirit may lead you to pray in a totally different dialect such as French, Japanese, Luo, or Swahili. When that happens, just flow with the Holy Spirit. Most likely you would be praying for nations or people who understand that language or prophesying and decreeing by the Holy Spirit in those languages.

One must pray loudly and be physically aggressive while praying in order to be effective in prayer. These too are not true. Recall from the previous chapter that it is the prayer of sincerity and of faith that gets God's attention. God searches the intents of the heart. *"I the Lord search the heart and examine the mind, to reward each person according to their conduct, according to what their deeds deserve"* (Jeremiah 17:10). Moreover, He knows our needs even before we ask. *"And when you pray, do not keep on babbling like pagans, for they think they will be heard because of their many words. Do not be like them, for your Father knows what you need before you ask him"* (Matthew 6:7-8 NKJV). So if our intentions are not pure in prayer, shouting and physical maneuvers will not bring answers. That is why the Bible warns that our prayers are not answers because we pray to meet our own desires and not God's desires for us. This is done when our intentions for prayer are wrong. *"When you ask, you do not receive, because you ask with wrong motives, that you may spend what you get on your pleasures"* (James 4.3 NKJV).

Also, we should be cautious not to mimic others or adopt religious cultural practices in order to be considered effective in prayer. From personal experience, I have observed believers who believe in acrobatics, shouting, and running around during prayer. Others believe that the louder they pray the more effective they are. Most of these are just learned behaviors or practices based on the religious culture one was raised in. Again these are not necessary. All prayers should be conducted in love, in faith, with boldness, most importantly with the Holy Spirit's leading. I will discuss the role of the Holy Spirit in the upcoming chapters.

Prayer is all about rebuking the devil, decreeing, declaring, and prophesying. When the prayer is directed by the Holy Spirit, He leads the prayer to the areas on which we need to focus. As believers, we pray from a position of victory so we should not constantly steer prayer to rebuking, binding, and casting. Granted, there are times when these are needed, but the key is not to focus on a defeated foe, Satan.

I am convinced that these are learned or taught behaviors that have cumulated to mindsets. Unless teaching and revelation is brought to such believers, they will continue in these patterns of prayer. Instead, we should we should acknowledge the Greater person we have in us and focus our prayer through the Holy Spirit on Christ who has overcome all. By this we therefore pray from "up looking down," not from "down looking up". I recommend reading *The Happy Intercessor* by Beni Johnson for more elaboration on praying from a position of victory.

Lastly, making declarations and prophesying are not wrong, but they must align with God's Word and purposes for us. When prayer is directed by the Holy Spirit, decrees, declarations, and prophesies also emanate from the Holy Spirit. The Holy Spirit will only release what is supported by the Word of God and what is in God's will. No wonder John warns to test all spirits because if decrees, declarations, and prophesies do not match the will and the Word of God, again we will be praying amiss. See the following from John 4:1-6:

> Beloved, do not believe every spirit, but test the spirits to see whether they are from God, for many false prophets have gone out into the world. By this you know the Spirit of God: every spirit that confesses that Jesus Christ has

come in the flesh is from God, and every spirit that does not confess Jesus is not from God. This is the spirit of the antichrist, which you heard was coming and now is in the world already. Little children, you are from God and have overcome them, for he who is in you is greater than he who is in the world. They are from the world; therefore, they speak from the world, and the world listens to them. We are from God. Whoever knows God listens to us; whoever is not from God does not listen to us. By this we know the Spirit of truth and the spirit of error. (NKJV)

One must recite pre-printed prayer or use prayer books in order to be effective in Prayer. I believe prayer books and manuals were written with the right intentions to support a believer's prayer life. These books can be used for guidance, reference, and training in prayer, but we should not rely on them solely as substitutes to prayer. As stated earlier, prayer is simply talking to God and communicating with God. Everybody should be in a position to talk to God at any time without utilizing a book or manual. If we are to stay dependent on these books, it would mean we cannot pray on the days we forget to carry them or if they get lost.

Utilize prayer books to gain knowledge. Use them where needed in various aspects of prayer. Just do not substitute them for prayer or be dependent on them as your only source of prayer. Also, do not forget that you have the ever-present Holy Spirit to help your prayer and give you specific areas of what you really need to pray for. The ever-present help in time of need that the Holy Spirit provides. Watch out! The Holy Spirit can prompt you to pray anytime, anywhere through any means.

There is a "lingo" or vocabulary for prayer. Using such language makes one effective in prayer. The source of this lie again comes through religion and learned behavior. Apart from the teaching Jesus gave His disciples about prayer, there is no special lingo or vocabulary that should be used in prayer. I am glad nowadays that most have transitioned from using King James English to pray, but I must caution that there still remain some rumblings that are not necessarily prayer. I am not referencing praying in the language of the Holy Spirit, which is also called, praying in tongues. I will discuss this in the upcoming chapters.

I have observed situations where a believer was so desperate to be filled with the gift of speaking in tongues and because she did not know how to go about it, she mimicked what the person praying next to her was doing. Now that can be excused, because it was done out of knowledge. I have also observed people shouting "fire, fire, fire" irrespective of what the prayer being led in was about. Most concerning though, I have witnessed false tongues being expressed during prayer. False tongues are satanic mimics of the real and true gift of speaking in tongues of the Holy Spirit.

All the points that I have discussed in this section are driven by the flesh and not the Spirit of God. From personal experience, such misconceptions normally exist in order to attract attention to one's self and present one's self as though effective in prayer. However, all these are amiss. Hence the title of this book. Just talk to God in the language you understand.

You need to have a specific place or time in order to pray. There is nothing wrong with identifying specific places or setting a time to pray. Daniel did this. He prayed with the window open three times a day. *"Now when Daniel knew that the writing was signed, he went home. And in his upper room, with his windows open toward Jerusalem, he knelt down on his knees three times* *that day, and prayed and gave thanks before his God, as was his custom since early days"* (Daniel 6:10 NKJV).

King David woke up early in the morning to seek God. In the New Testament, we read several accounts where Jesus retreated to pray. Most of the time He went to the mountains, but he also went to Mount Olive as well as Gethsemane. Cornelius a covert to Christianity is also mentioned to have prayed in the afternoon around 3:00 p.m. (Acts 10:30 NKJV).

Although these examples indicate specification of time, praying is not restricted to designated times of the day. It is good to set aside times out of discipline, commitment to God, and desire for intimacy with God; however, prayer can be done at any time. We should anticipate and practice praying at anytime and anywhere. This revelation came after a period of recognizing our authority as believers in Christ and the omnipresent nature of our God. God is present wherever we are and hears us in whatever condition we are in.

Moreover, once saved and filled, the Holy Christ and the Holy Spirit live in us; they never leave. This means, we can exercise our right and power in prayer wherever we are: in the car, while shopping, on a plane, in the office, in the late hours of the night, and even in the shower! Christ's power in us is not limited to a space or time. Subsequently, since the Father and the Son are one, the omnipresent nature of God allows Him to be everywhere and timeless. This also means that we can even pray subconsciously while sleeping and silently with only our minds, talking to God without opening our mouths.

Prayer must be audible. The fact that we can pray silently negates the other misconception that we ought to be loud and physically aggressive in prayer in order for God to hear our prayers. Prayer can be done audibly, quietly, and subconsciously. Effective prayer does not have to be audible. This applies more so to the current lifestyles, especially recognizing believers in the market place, those in schools, or those who may not have set places to pray. I am a strong advocate that each believer should have set private prayer at least twice a day. If one has the ability to do this, then sure, go ahead and be vocal in your prayer, but if you cannot pray audibly, silent prayers are equally heard by God.

The longer you pray the more God hears your Prayers. I used to struggle with this belief about prayer until eight years ago when I watched a teaching by Joyce Meyer on prayer. Before then, I believed that praying for longer periods of time was impressive to God and to an extent validated me as a prayerful believer. It from this teaching that I pursued studying more about prayer, specifically praying by faith. I am not endorsing prayerlessness or five-minute prayers while out the door on the way to work or emergency prayers when crises occur. I believe God responds to the prayer of faith rather than a longer, faithless prayer.

It is important to set time for prayer and allow the Holy Spirit to lead the prayer. When you grant the Holy Spirit that time, He will set the start time and the end time. From personal experience though, the Holy Spirit always wants to show you more and pray more through you. With time, I have come to recognize that the Holy Spirit prays through me a lot in silence, especially while I'm at work. I have also experienced a time while driving and making a right turn, I burst out praying in tongues audibly for a short period of time, then resumed back to just singing.

So stay flexible with when and where the Spirit chooses to pray with you. Also realize that you can pray without opening your mouth when your mind, heart, spirit, and the Holy Spirit are synchronized in prayer. If you push through your fatigue, He will strengthen you to pray more with Him. However; I want to encourage you to pray believing that God heard you, whether you only have a second to pray or four hours to pray. Prayer is not a matter of works and length of prayer, but rather by faith and belief in God.

You must have prayer points in order to be effective in prayer. Based on observation and experience in attending some prayer meetings, a prayer point is a topic specifying an area of focus while praying. It can be defined as what to pray from. In some religious circles, these prayer points are usually associated with a scripture with mostly key words pulled from the scripture and used as a focus area or prayer point to pray. From observation, however, the majority of these prayer points are usually applied to spiritual warfare prayers. Additionally, such prayers are normally repeated several times and emphasized during prayer. Finally, most of these prayer points are normally introverted, in that the prayers are centered towards "I," "Me," or "Mine." Rarely are they related to what God should do *with* the person, and they instead focus on what God should do *for* the person.

Prayer points in themselves are not wrong. In fact, it is preferred that we approach God with specific things we want to pray for. It is also good to establish structure in prayer. The Lord's Prayer was very organized and to the point. The issue is not to solely rely on the prayer points for prayer. Instead, seek the assistance of the Holy Spirit and ask Him to lead your prayers. The Holy Spirit is the all-knowing God in us. He prays with groaning and in languages that we do not understand. The Holy Spirit knows our hearts as well as the heart of God. What better Person to ask to assist and guide you in prayer than the Holy Spirit?

I will share how I approach God in prayer. When I am ready to petition God during prayer, I normally present my list to the Lord and say, *"Holy Spirit we (Pauline and the Holy Spirit) are praying about these, please take over this prayer."* From there I just let the Holy Spirit direct the prayer, whether it is in understanding or in tongues. Try doing this the next time you are praying. Pay attention to any specific things you did not even plan to pray about that come out of your mouth. In such times know that the Holy Spirit has taken over the prayer. He will astound you! I encourage you to write down the specific things that the Holy Spirit prayed about after completing prayer. Make a habit of placing a journal next to you during prayer. Later reflect and meditate on what you wrote down. God normally speaks to us during prayers. From experience, new things are birthed by the Holy Spirit during prayer. Destinies and plans are clarified, and impartations and anointing occurs.

God does a lot during prayer. Be careful with solely focusing on prayer points. This creates rigidity and leans more towards works of the flesh, which are powerless and faithless prayers. Instead, be flexible and allow the free flow of the Holy Spirit in your prayers.

You need a specific person in order to pray or to be prayed for. On two separate occasions my friends shared with me that believers had come to them saying, "I do not want anyone else to pray for me except you," referencing my friends. "Whenever you pray I get answers, and that is why I want you pray for me." This false belief only leaves people prayer-less, faithless, on the verge of idolatry, and subject to exploitation by false teachers.

If you recall from previous chapters on "Aspects of Prayer," I explained that as Christians we pray to the Only God, one God. Entrusting someone else to do anything for us means we have removed our focus from the Creator (God) to His creation (woman or man). Doing this is idolatry, the worship of someone or something other than God. It also shows that we do not trust God but we live in our own understanding; the understanding being that only "so and so" can pray for us.

Throughout the Bible, there are numerous warnings against putting our trust away from God. The verse that comes to mind right now is Proverbs 3:5-6: *"Trust in the Lord with all your heart and lean not on your own understanding; in all your ways submit to him, and he will make your paths straight."* (NKJV). The key point from this scripture is "trust with all your heart." Remember in previous chapters I discussed God searching the intents of our hearts. The other point is "lean not in your own understanding." Leaning on our own understanding translates to works of the flesh. The works here being the false belief that prayers only get answered when specific people pray.

The most disturbing trend that I have observed is the increase of false teachers who say that they can pray for others but only do so if a financial seed is sown to them. Such teachers identify themselves with titles, the most preferred one being "prophet." In disguise they exploit a lot of vulnerable people who are hurting or wounded and are desperate for breakthrough. Most often targeted are single women or women in general. Sadly, some believers have even designated then as their "personal prophets" whom they contact and remit money to regularly for prayers. The other problem with this practice is that most believers do even know these so called prophets or prophetesses since their locations are either kept discrete or they live out of town or even in a different country. I caution you that dependence on such false teachers has the greater potential of being financially exploited, and spiritually, emotionally, physically, and even sexually abused.

Be very careful with anyone who asks you for money or favors in order to pray for you. Be very careful of anyone who is very secretive; who wants to know your affairs and never discloses themselves to you. Avoid dealing with people you do not fully know, especially if they are long distance. There are countless stories about believers who have suffered at the hands of these prayer acquaintances. Most may not be praying for you anyway, so leave them alone and have your own prayer life! Certainly, if you are totally sowing into these persons, and you end up more depleted in any way rather than being edified, this should be clear sign that you have entrusted the wrong person. In addition to the anointing, someone's character and lifestyle also matters. If the fruits of the Spirit and the character of Christ are not evidenced consistently in someone, then you may be dealing with a wrong person.

To combat the false belief of needing someone to pray for you or designating a "prayer prophetess or prophet," believe in God, believe in His Word, and also believe in yourself. Greater is He that is in you than He that is the word. Secondly, you have the Trinity living in you: God the Father, God the Son, God the Holy Spirit. For any Spirit filled believer, you have the power pack of these Three, the God Head living in you as the Person of the Holy Spirit! With Him and in Him you can independently pray without constantly relying on others to do it for you. Granted there are times that you need support from fellow believers, intercessors, prayer partners, pastors, and true prophets and prophetesses. However, this should not be a habit. There are times we have to overcome laziness and take personal responsibility of our walk with God. This includes taking responsibility to pray intentionally for ourselves, by ourselves, and with help of the Holy Spirit.

Change tone of voice or assume a particular posture in order to pray effectively. Have you ever observed this? When someone is called to pray, all of the sudden they change their tone of voice and even posture before they start to pray. The tone is normally low and soft. At times the hands are folded, eyes closed, etc. Depending on upbringing, some may have been taught doing this is reverencing God and humbling, because "we should come to God with a humble spirit."

The above is true, but I encourage you to come and approach God as you are in prayer. Talk to God as you would talk to a friend. By the way, God calls you "friend" in John 15:15, *"No longer do I call you servants, for a servant does not know what his master is doing; but I have called you friends, for all things that I heard from My Father I have made known to you."* (NKJV). You do not change your posture or tone while talking to a genuine friend, so why do that when it comes to communicating to and with God, your Friend? Moreover, God also calls us sons and daughters. So, we talk to Him freely, without fear, just as we talk to our parents.

WHY SHOULD WE PRAY?

†

A believer's lifestyle should encompass regular prayer. There are several reasons why we pray. Below are some of the reasons, but bear in mind that even though there may be more reasons than the ones listed, I will attempt to exhaust the list. We pray . . .

● *As a means of communication with God our Father.* Prayer is communication to God. Prayer is the most important means of communicating to God. As sons, daughters, and friends of God, we have to establish a relationship with. Though God knows us, and we slightly know Him, He longs to expose Himself to us and tell more about Himself and more about us as well. We pray to get this relationship going. It is through prayer that we know the heart of God. The relationship gets stronger as we seek continually to communicate through praying, just as it would grow in a healthy relationship.

In the following scriptures, God is calling us to this relationship. One of the ways of seeking God is by communicating to Him. *"You will seek me and find me if you seek Me out of clean heart"* (Jeremiah 29: 13 NKJV). *"Seek the Lord while He may be found. Call on Him while He is near"* (Isaiah 55.6 NKJV).

● *So that we may not be tempted or fall into temptation.* Jesus Christ, in His teachings, warned us that in the world there would be many tribulations, but to fear not because He overcame for us (John 33:16 NKJV). Tribulations and unbelief are two things that can lead us into temptation. In order to avoid temptation, we must pray. So we pray to avoid temptation. Jesus teaches this in Mark 14:38: *"Watch and pray that you may not enter into temptation. The spirit indeed* *is willing, but the flesh is weak." (NKJV)*By this, we know that temptations can be avoided when we pray.

● *For our needs to be meet.* Although God is our Father and He gives liberally, God still desires that we ask Him for what we need. God offers to meet our needs as the Creator of all things as well as the One who knows the desires of our hearts. Think of it as our Father. He is also best left to know what is good for us. This makes God our ultimate supplier of all needs. We should seek God and not humans, things, or money to meet our needs. He says we will receive what we ask for.

In the petition portion of the prayer, we do the asking. Remember, petitioning is making a formal request. It is through prayer that we make known our requests to God. The Bible teaches that *"whatever things you ask in prayer, believing, you will receive."* (Matthew 21:22 NKJV). The prayer of petition may vary in the type of need being requested. Whichever way, God guarantees to respond. *"Ask, and it will be given to you; seek, and you will find; knock, and it will be opened to you. For everyone who asks receives, and he who seeks finds, and to him who knocks it will be opened"* (Matthew 7: 7-8 NKJV).

● *For the care of one another.* We are one body united to and by One Head—Jesus Christ. The foundation of this unity is built in love, the love for one another and the love for God. 1 Corinthians 12:25-27 calls for each believer to have mutual concern for one another because of this unity. Because of this, when one believer suffers we suffer with him/her, when one rejoices, we rejoice with him/her.

Prayer is one of the ways we express this care, love, and support for one another. Apostle Paul in his letters to the Ephesian church and to Timothy instructs us on this. *"Praying always with all prayer and supplication in the Spirit, and watching thereunto with all perseverance and supplication for all saints"* (Ephesians: 6:18 NKJV). *"I exhort therefore, that, first of all, supplications, prayers, intercessions, and thanksgiving be made for all men"* (1 Timothy 2:1 NKJV).

♦ *For a country's peace or national peace.* There is such power in the individual or collective intercession for a country and for all nations. After living in an area for song, I recently received a revelation that God had assigned me as an intercessor for that region. In fact, the revelation went further. The Holy Spirit showed me that God designates the locations we live in to impact and influence that geographical location with His presence though us! Halleluiah. This is when I learned the importance of seeking God and allowing Him to strategically assign us believers where to live. God is into every detail of our lives. The Holy Spirit then opened my eyes and showed me fellow believers who had miraculous breakthroughs purchasing homes. Then, He proceeded to whisper that each received these miracles to be staged as intercessors covering miles and miles away.

So, in whatever country, city, business, or place of employment you are in, you have an influence there. One of which is prayer. So pray for your peace and the needs for your house, neighborhood, city, and nation. You never know the impact of those prayers and the vast geographical area your prayers will impact. The Bible instructs us to pray for our nations and rulers: *"I exhort therefore, that, first of all, supplications, prayers, intercessions, and thanksgiving be made for all men; for kings, and for all that are in authority; that we may lead a quiet and peaceable life in all godliness and honesty. For this is good and accept able in the sight of God our Savior"* (1 Timothy 2:1-3 NKJV).

♦ *To receive God's blessings.* The prayer of Jabez comes to mind. Jabez was not afraid to cry to God. He cried out, prayed fervently to God, and God blessed him. Jabez was very specific in the blessings he wanted from God. He prayed

"Oh that you would bless me and enlarge my territory! Let your hand be with me, and keep me from harm so that I will be free from pain" (1 Chronicles 4:10 NKJV). God granted his request.

David had multiple prayers for blessings in the book of Psalms. In them David shows that when we seek God in prayer, He blesses us. *"He will receive blessings from the Lord and vindication from God His savior. Such is the generation of those who seek Him. Who seek Your face of God of Jacob?"* (Psalm 24:5-6 NKJV).

". . . Those who seek the Lord lack no good thing" (Psalm 34:10 NKJV). Whenever I have thoughts of a delayed breakthrough or answer to my prayers, this is one of the verses that anchors me. That God will never withhold any good thing that He designated for me to reach me. So I normally remind God of this verse in prayer as well thank Him for the good blessings and stand on this promise after praying until the blessings come.

♦ *To Change the outcome of a negative situation or to change a negative destiny.* There are countless examples in the Bible where God altered the outcomes of adversarial conditions when people called on Him. Let us start with Abraham who debated with God several times to save the righteous in Sodom and Gomorrah and God did, by rescuing Lot's family. Followed by Jacob who demanded that the angel bless him when he wrestled with the angel. Here Jacob experience his destiny changed characterized by the change of his name from Jacob to Israel. Then, we have Joshua who prayed for the sun to stand still in the valley of Aijalon so that his army may continue to war. We later we see David and Esther have great victories as they lead the people to prayer and later plans of their enemies.

How about Jabez, whom we mentioned previously. Apparently, he was born in pain according to his mother (1 Chronicles 4:9 NKJV). In studies, I've learned that children often lived what they were named. That is why Jacob's name had to change from swindler to Israel. Jabez in realizing this said "no way." He petitioned God in prayer, crying out *let your hand be with me, and keep me from harm so that I will be free from pain*" (1 Chronicles 4:10 NKJV). God granted his request.

The Bible account I love the most, and I love the entire Bible don't get me wrong, but Hezekiah's account really exemplifies the power of changing destiny through prayer. From these accounts I learned that although he had such great power as king, Hezekiah did not rely on his own authority. In the two instances that Hezekiah received negative reports, he turned to God for help. Hezekiah submitted to God through prayer. 2 Kings 20:1-6(NKJV) states that *When King Hezekiah was told that he was going to die from an illness, his first reaction was a turn towards the wall and prayed. He changed the outcome of the bad news by refusing to accept it and sort God for mercy in prayer."*

In turn, this is how God responded to Hezekiah's prayer. This is what the Lord says: *"Put your house in order, because you are going to die; you will not recover. Hezekiah turned his face to the wall and prayed to the Lord, 'Remember, Lord, how I have walked before you faithfully and with wholehearted devotion and have done what is good in your eyes.' And Hezekiah wept bitterly. Then the word of the Lord came to Isaiah: 'Go and tell Hezekiah, this is what the Lord, the God of your father David, says: I have heard your prayer and seen your tears; I will add fifteen years to your life.'"* (Isaiah 38:1-5 NKJV). God healed King Hezekiah and extended fifteen more years of good health and life to him.

Prior to this, King Hezekiah had been threatened by another nation that blasphemed God and wanted to wage war with the King. This time King Hezekiah received the letter, read it, and went and spread the letter before the

Lord in prayer. Because of his prayer, the Lord sent His Own Angel to fight the Assyrians. The Lord also restored Hezekiah's kingdom. Hezekiah received the letter from the messengers and read it. Then he went up to the temple of the Lord and spread it out before the Lord. *"And Hezekiah prayed to the Lord"* (2 Kings 19 NKJV). Here again Hezekiah changed the destiny of a nation by praying.

♦ *For Healing and Forgiveness.* 2 Chronicles 7:14 is a commonly quoted scripture in times of corporate or individual consecration. In this scripture, we also learn another aspect of humility, which is prayer. The humility here is of the mind, heart, and body. I believe it also means the intents of the heart.

It is prayer that we can humble ourselves and ask God for repentance. When this happens, God responds by not only forgiving us but also by healing us. *"If My people who are called by My name will humble themselves, and pray and seek My face, and turn from their wicked ways, then I will hear from heaven, and will forgive their sin and heal their land"* (2 Chronicles 7:14 NKJV). The healing that God brings from such prayers go beyond physical healing. Healing here may include spiritual, emotional, and/or mental healing. Healing may come in form of restored relationships, restored finances or business venture. Healing may also come in form of a breakthrough or solution to a problem.

♦ *To mend relationships with one another.* God is relational and so are His children. As the body of Christ we should strive for peace amongst ourselves. In fact, the Scripture directs us to be at peace with everyone. *"If it is possible, as much as depends on you, live peaceably with all men"* (Romans 12:18 NKJV). However, we cannot control everything about mankind. Therefore, misunderstandings and conflicts may indivertibly occur. These have tendencies create offenses and change relationships.

The antidote to these is asking each other for forgiveness then praying for one another. The scripture that directs us to do so is James 5:16: *"Confess your trespasses (sins) to one another, and pray for one another, that you may be healed." (NKJV).* The effective, fervent prayer of a righteous man avails much. Confessing our sins to one another also opens a platform for accountability; where we can be open to each other but also hold each other accountable and accept constructive scriptural correction from one another.

Reconciliation with one another is a prerequisite to approaching God with any form of prayer. Again, God is looking at the conditions of our hearts and our motives before we approach Him for anything, whether in prayer or service. This is a reminder that whatever comes to God cannot be defiled. Our prayers and praises must be pure and holy before him. Hence God directs that *"if you are offering your gift at the altar and there remember that your brother or sister has something against you, leave your gift there in front of the altar. First go and be reconciled to them; then come and offer your gift"* (Matthew 5:23-24 NKJV).

Reconciliation, asking one another for forgiveness, and holding each other accountable may be difficult, but be bold and take the initial step. In fact, I would encourage you to take the first step towards reconciliation even when you know you are a thousand percent right and the other party is totally wrong! For one, it reflects a level of maturity, and most importantly, you are responsible for what God tells you to do! So approach the person, ask to be forgiven of the offense or misunderstanding, if any, and do not get into deeper clarification or much explanation. From personal experience, at times doing this just makes the situation worse. Try to explain yourself, but do not force it if you sense resistance or if the person keeps focusing on the negatives, condemns you, or tries to inflict guilt, especially after you have repented to them.

It is also crucial as part of confession and reconciliation to evaluate your role in the situation. Be a good listener instead, and do not try to justify your actions. From personal experience, I have learned that there are always underlying issues behind people's offenses. A hurting person hurts, an offended person offends, a deeply wounded person wounds, a fearful person inflicts fear, an insecure person attempts to control or manipulate. An orange tree produces oranges. Ask the Holy Spirit to show you the root of the issues and how to deal or tell the person. Also ask the Holy Spirit for the timing to do the reconciliation. Face to face interaction is preferred, but if you can, use any forum to initiate conversation. Do not allow unforgiveness, offenses, bitterness, and even pain to hinder your prayers or affect your prayer life. I highly recommend a small booklet by Kenneth Copeland on *Offenses*. The other remarkable book I recommend is *Strengthen Yourself in the Lord* by Bill Johnson.

◆ *To ask for the fullness of God.* Once saved, we go through stages of development in our faith and our knowledge about God and the Holy Spirit. All of us are created in God's image, and God desires that we attain that full image; coming to full maturity in Him so that we may be one in God and one with Christ. This, the prayer Jesus prayed for us towards the end of His life on earth. Here is the prayer Jesus prayed for us in John 17:9-11: *"I pray for them. I do not pray for the world but for those whom You have given Me, for they are Yours. And all Mine are Yours, and Yours are Mine, and I am glorified in them. Now I am no longer in the world, but these are in the world, and I come to You. Holy Father, keep through Your name those whom You have given Me, that they may be one as We are one." (NKJV)*

There is more that God wants to do us, with us and through us. We have just scratched the surface. Prayer is one the foundational ways to attain this fullness. The prayer of faith, in love, out of compassion, obedience, and submission to the Holy Spirit, are also essential. The key requirement though is prayer. "Ask and it shall be given to you!" Meaning pray asking for this fullness! *"Ask, and it will be given to you; seek, and you will find; knock, and it will be opened to you. For everyone who asks receives, and he who seeks finds, and to him who knocks it will be opened"* (Matthew 7: 7-8 NKJV).

Prayer is the door to experiencing the fullness of God. In the epistles, written by Apostle Paul, you will notice over and over Paul praying different prayers for the churches, his mentees, and for the saints. Among Paul's prayers that I reference often is the prayer in Ephesians 3:14-19:

> *For this reason I bow my knees to the Father of our Lord Jesus Christ, from whom the whole family in heaven and earth is named, that He would grant you, according to the riches of His glory, to be strengthened with might through His Spirit in the inner man, that Christ may dwell in your hearts through faith; that you, being rooted and grounded in love, may be able to comprehend with all the saints what is the width and length and depth and height to know the love of Christ which passes knowledge; that you may be filled with all the fullness of God. (NKJV)*

♦ *To be filled with The Holy Spirit.* The promise of the outpour of the Holy Spirit was based on a directive from Jesus Christ for His disciples to wait in the upper room. While they were there praying on the day of Pentecost, suddenly they were filled by the Holy Spirit. Another example that associates prayer and the move of the Holy Spirit is in Acts 8:15 and Acts 8:17 when Peter and John went to minister to new converts in Samaria. When they arrived, *"they prayed for the new believers there that they might receive the Holy Spirit."* (NKJV). Then Peter and John placed their hands on them, and they received the Holy Spirit. By these, we see that prayer is the catalyst to the move of the Holy Spirit.

Repeatedly throughout the entire Bible, you will notice that a mighty move of God or in-filling of the Holy Spirit was preceded by prayer. Consider Pentecost *"When the Day of Pentecost had fully come, they were all with one accord in one place. And suddenly there came a sound from heaven, as of a rushing mighty wind, and it filled the whole house where they were sitting. Then there appeared to them divided tongues, as of fire, and one sat upon each of them. And they were all filled with the Holy Spirit and began to speak with other tongues, as the Spirit gave them utterance"* (Acts 2:1-4 NKJV). Peter was released from prison because believers were gathered praying for him (Acts 12:5-17 NKJV). Paul and Barnabas were selected and sent to preach the gospel following a period of fasting and praying that was done by the apostles. *"While they were worshiping the Lord and fasting, the Holy Spirit said, 'Set apart for me Barnabas and Saul for the work to which I have called them'"* (Acts 13:2 NKJV).

While in prison, Paul and Silas were released miraculously, after they had praised and worshipped, a form of prayer. Here is the testimony of their prayer: *"But at midnight Paul and Silas were praying and singing hymns to God, and the prisoners were listening to them. Suddenly there was a great earthquake, so that the foundations of the prison were shaken; and immediately all the doors were opened and everyone's chains were loosed"* (Acts 16:25-26 NKJV).

God always moves when we pray. Personally, I experience powerful impartations and intense communion with the Holy Spirit while praying or immediately after ending the prayer. Prayer activates the move of God and the move of the Holy Spirit!

To seek God's guidance and direction. More and more I am learning the importance of total submission to God and seeking God first in everything. It is true that when we acknowledge God's supremacy and rely on Him, God provides much better outcomes than we do. The Bible has innumerable accounts of kings, servants, and women who sought God first for guidance before they ventured into war of leadership. Joshua, David, Hezekiah, and Nehemiah are examples. Most kings of the Old Testament sought God's direction also through prophets. However, the most intriguing prayer was King Solomon's. Shortly after being enthroned as the new king of Israel, Solomon sought the Lord in prayer by asking God for wisdom to guide his new kingdom. Solomon's prayer covers all aspects of prayer that are discussed in the earlier chapters of this book. See if you can identify those aspects in the following scriptures. Most importantly look for the intent of Solomon's heart and the humility he submitted to in asking God for guidance. The scriptures are from 2 Chronicles 2:6-12:

> *Solomon went up to the bronze altar before the Lord in the tent of meeting and offered a thousand burnt offerings on it. That night God appeared to Solomon and said to him, "Ask for whatever you want me to give you." Solomon answered God, "You have shown great kindness to David my father and have made me king in his place. Now, Lord God, let your promise to my father David be confirmed, for you have made me king over a people who are as numerous as the dust of the earth. Give me wisdom and knowledge, that I may lead this people, for who is able to govern this great people of yours?" God said to Solomon, "Since this is your heart's desire and you have not asked for wealth, possessions or honor, nor for the death of your enemies, and since you have not asked for a long life but for wisdom and knowledge to govern my people over whom I have made you king, therefore wisdom and knowledge will be given you. And*

I will also give you wealth, possessions and honor, such as no king who was before you ever had and none after you will have." (NKJV)

In the New Testament we see the disciples of Jesus or apostles seek direction through prayer and fasting. *"Commit your way to the Lord, Trust also in Him, And He shall bring it to pass. He shall bring forth your righteousness as the light, and your justice as the noonday"* (Psalm 37:5-7 NKJV). *"I will instruct you and teach you in the way should go; I will guide you with my eye"* (Psalm 32:8 NKJV).

• *As part of spiritual warfare.* Spiritual warfare is not limited to prayer. The best way to describe spiritual warfare it that it is a lifestyle that incorporates prayer. By a lifestyle, I mean wearing the full armor of God constantly. The full armor involves standing and staying strong, walking in truth and transparency to one another, having the breastplate of righteousness which is love and faith, being ready to share the gospel, constantly walking in faith, guarding our minds by setting our minds on the things of God because through salvation we are the mind of Christ, utilizing and applying the Word of God as our sword and finally praying in Spirit and praying for all people. We see how prayer becomes and a significant part of spiritual warfare according to Ephesians 6:10-18.

Once born again or saved, our lives are transformed to the image of Christ. Our Christian walk then becomes a spiritual one, not one detected by our mind, soul, or body. We are spiritual beings in fleshly bodies, and we relate to a Spiritual God. The oppositions we face are also spiritual. Satan and his demons are spiritual beings who inhabit bodies or objects. This means that to combat Satan we must approach him in the spirit not through the flesh. That is why Apostle Paul wrote that we wrestle not through flesh and body but against spiritual forces. This why Paul instructs us to pray in the Spirit in Ephesians 6:18, *"and pray in the Spirit on all occasions with all kinds of prayers and requests."* (NKJV)

Prayer is one of the armors utilized to wrestle against satanic operations. Usually this is called spiritual warfare prayer. *"Finally, my brethren, be strong in the Lord and in the power of His might. Put on the whole armor of God that you may be able to stand against the wiles of the devil. For we do not wrestle against flesh and blood, but against principalities, against powers, against the rulers of the darkness of this age, against spiritual hosts of wickedness in the heavenly places. Therefore, take up the whole armor of God that you may be able to withstand in the evil day, and having done all, to stand."* (NKJV) Verse 18 emphasizes praying always with all prayer and supplication in the Spirit, being watchful to this end with all perseverance and supplication for all the saints.

BE REAL. OPEN UP TO GOD IN PRAYER

†

This chapter discusses the relational nature that God has with us, His children. As sons, daughters, and as friends of God, we have the freedom to talk to God directly and freely. I believe the reason why most believers do not pray is because of guilt and condemnation. Satan can falsely convince people that God is a condemning God and only deals with us from a punitive perspective. The other reason for distancing ourselves from God by not praying is the false belief that God is too far to reach or to hear our prayers. Most damaging is the lie that Satan often feeds believers, which is that God is mad at us because of a delay in answering a prayer. Therefore, most believers shut down and do not pray at all.

The Bible is filled with countless promises of the assurance of forgiveness by God and experiencing freedom in Christ Jesus. Psalm 103 is a favorite chapter that I often reference when it comes to guilt free living as a child of God. Here are some verses that affirm your guilt free position:

- Psalm 103:2-4: *"Bless the Lord, O my soul, and forget not all His benefits: Who forgives all your iniquities, Who heals all your diseases, Who redeems your life from destruction, Who crowns you with lovingkindness and tender mercies." (NKJV)*

- Psalm 103:8-10: *"The Lord is merciful and gracious, slow to anger, and abounding in mercy. He will not always strive with us, nor will He keep His anger forever. He has not dealt with us according to our sins, nor punished us according to our iniquities." (NKJV)*

- Psalm 103:11-13: *"For as the heavens are high above the earth, so great is His mercy toward those who fear Him; As far as the east is from the west, so far has He removed our transgressions from us. As a father pities his children, So the Lord pities those who fear Him." (NKJV)*

◆ Hebrews 8:12: *"For I will be merciful regarding their wrong deeds, and I will never again remember their sins." (NKJV)*

◆ Isaiah 43:25: *"I even I, am the one who wipes out your transgressions for My own sake, And I will not remember your sins." (NKJV)*

If you have been taught such or convinced that God has not forgiven your sins after repenting, all these are demonic lies to hinder your walk with God and to hinder you from praying. No sin is too big to negate praying. As born again believers we have been set free from guilt, condemnation, or fear. The Blood Jesus Christ was shed, His death and resurrection, gave us free access to God. Because of these, *"let us therefore come boldly to the throne of grace, that we may obtain mercy and find grace to help in time of need"* (Hebrews 4:16 NKJV).

Approach God with boldness because you are no longer guilty

God's love for us, through the redemptive blood of Jesus, also makes us accepted by Him without guilt or condemnation. Roman 8:1-2 is an assuring promise: *"therefore, there is now no condemnation for those who are in Christ Jesus,"* (NKJV) because through Christ Jesus the law of the Spirit who gives life has set you free from the law of sin and death. We can approach God boldly because He has given us the liberty to relate to God freely and openly.

Scriptures further reiterate that we reign with Christ. We are seated at the right hand of the Father. We are coheirs with Christ, a chosen generation, a royal priesthood, and holy nation. With such designations, we have every right to approach God freely. *"But ye are a chosen generation, a royal priesthood, a holy nation, a peculiar people; that ye should shew forth the praises of him who hath called you out of darkness into his marvelous light"* (Peter 2:9 NKJV).

Seeing then that we have a great High Priest who has passed through the heavens, Jesus the Son of God, let us hold fast our confession. *"For we do not have a High Priest who cannot sympathize with our weaknesses, but was in all points tempted as we are, yet without sin. Let us therefore come boldly to the throne of grace that we may obtain mercy and find grace to help in time of need"* (Hebrews 4:14-16 NKJV).

Approach God with love because God is love

God relates to us through the eyes of love, and that is how we should relate back to Him. With the understanding that prayer is our way of communicating and establishing relationship with God, we must relate and communicate out of love and desire to want to know Him more. Communicating and serving God out of love for Him changes our approach and attitude towards prayer from requesting things from God like a "want list" to a greater depth of intimacy. With love as the foundation of prayer, there is more openness and transparency with God. As you pour out unconditionally, God also reveals His heart to you. Praying out of love changes us from "God do for me" to "God do in me and do through me."

This love connection through prayer draws us more closely to God. A new hunger for His presence develops; God draws us to Him. God relates with us in true love. In Jeremiah 31:1 and 31:3 it states, *"'At the same time,' says the Lord, 'I will be the God of all the families of Israel, and they shall be my people.' The Lord has appeared of old to me, saying: 'Yes, I have loved you with an everlasting love; therefore, with lovingkindness I have drawn you."* (NKJV) When done out of love, praying becomes effortless because it is love that draws us to want to talk to God.

Additionally, God has called us with lovingkindness, so that when we approach Him in prayer, we approach Him from a position of love, knowing that He loves us and there is no fear in approaching Him. God is love. And so we know and rely on the love God has for us. Whoever lives in love lives in God, and God in them. This is how love is made complete among us so that we will have confidence on the Day of Judgment. In this world we are like Jesus. *"There is no fear in love. But perfect love drives out fear, because fear has to do with punishment. The one who fears is not made perfect in love"* (1 John 4:16-18 NKJV).

Approach God with sincere heart and mind

God is relational, and He desires that we serve Him in truth, in Spirit, and in righteousness. This involves sincerity in everything we do including prayer. As I indicated in previous chapters, our motives for prayer must be in accordance to God's purposes for us, not for selfish gain. Personally, I have learned to examine the issue I want to present to God in prayer, especially if it relates to a need or desire.

The other side of this applies to us; approaching God freely with the understanding that God examines the intents of the heart and the soul. God knows our hearts, so we cannot hide anything from Him. The response to our prayers depends on the fact that God is aware of our actual intentions. We certainly do not want to pray and not receive answers to our prayers because we are praying amiss. *"I, the Lord, search the heart, I test the mind, even to give every man according to his ways, according to the fruit of his doings"* (Jeremiah 17:10 NKJV).

Approach with an open heart and mind and tell it all

For a long time, I thought I was limited to what I could tell God in prayer. Therefore, although I had a pressing need or something bothered me, I often thought that the issues were inappropriate to present in prayer. It was not until 2009 that I received a revelation from Jeremiah 17:10 that God sees the intentions of the heart. Furthermore, the Holy Spirit reiterated that God is the one who created us, which makes Him even more qualified to know everything about us. If this same God knew us before we were born, if He already predestined us as His children, don't you think He knows everything about us? From that point on in 2009, I recall the exact place in the living room when I received this revelation; it was mid -morning between 10 a.m. and 11 a.m. when I began to speak my mind and heart freely to God.

The best approach is to talk to God freely without holding anything back. Of course, we still must reverence God and approach Him with respect and honor, but learn to talk or pray to God as though you were talking to a close friend. Maybe it helps to know that Jesus calls us friends according to John 15:15: *"I no longer call you servants, because a servant does not know his master's business. Instead, I have called you friends, for everything that I learned from my Father I have made known to you."* (NKJV) Learn to tell God in prayer exactly how you feel, how much it hurts, how excited you are, what your concerns are, etc. Just tell God.

Personally, I approach God like that. When someone makes me mad, I just pray: *"God I am so angry about what he/ she just did, please help me get this anger out."* Or, *"God he/she really offended me, I am hurt I have forgiven them but am still struggling with this, please help me forgive them. Holy Spirit show me how to deal with them when I see them next."* There was a period that I went through major adversity, pain, and trauma. During those periods, the pain was so deep that I could not utter words in prayer. Whenever I knelt to pray, I just cried till I could not cry any longer. I could conclude with "Amen" and get up for work. I believe that God heard my cries and with time I received healing. *"The righteous cry out, and the LORD hears them; he delivers them from all their troubles"* (Psalm 34:17 NKJV).

Talk to God, pray in the language YOU understand

Once you know that you can approach God freely, the misconceptions or "prayer manners," go out the window. You are free to talk or cry your heart out to God. It does not matter what language or order the prayers comes through. Just be real with God, talk to Him in the language YOU understand!

If you messed up, tell God exactly that. Say, *"Lord I messed up. I am angry. Lord, I am so mad I am about to slap somebody. Lord, I'm so hurt I cannot take it anymore. Lord, I need you to come through on this issue. Help me Lord. Lord, I am so excited, thank you."*

Be free with God and talk to Him respectfully in the language you know best including your native language, if you have one. Freedom with God frees us also. This is the liberty in Christ that in Him we are free indeed. This freedom is the freedom to speak our hearts and our minds. It by confessing that salvation comes; salvation in this context means breakthrough or answer. *"For with the heart one believes unto righteousness, and with the mouth confession is made unto salvation."* (Romans 10:10 NKJV). Receive your breakthrough, deliverance, and salvation.

Ask God what you do not know; Ask God questions

The Scriptures in Matthew 7:7-8 pertain to asking God about everything. The asking here is not limited to what we do not have but also what we do not understand. *"Ask, and it will be given to you; seek, and you will find; knock, and it will be opened to you. For everyone who asks receives, and he who seeks finds, and to him who knocks it will be opened."* (NKJV) All that is left for us to do is to inquire of the Lord.

During prayer or whenever you have a conversation with God, feel free to ask Him what you do not understand. Ask God to give you more details, to clarify the information you have read or received. I find this very helpful if God communicates to you through trances, visions, or dreams. Often God can provide different messages in one vision or dream. It is wonderful to know that we can return to God and ask the Holy Spirit to explain what we saw.

The other area in which I have found asking to be critical is the area of relationships, especially when I am about to enter into a contractual agreement or even just start a relationship with a person. I normally pray: *"God expose this person to me."* God normally answers this prayer in various forms. At times it through dreams and visions, and at other times it is through character traits and behaviors of the person. Most of the time what God shows in the dream is later confirmed by the person's behaviors and character. As I reflect back on my life, I realize that I would have saved a lot of heartache, disappointment, and money, if I only would have asked God some questions.

Jeremiah 33:3 is another affirming Scripture that I usually reflect on when it comes to asking. Here the Lord speaks to us saying, *"Call to Me, and I will answer you, and show you great and mighty things, which you do not know."* (NKJV). I gather from this scripture that we can ask God about our personal lives and lives of our loved ones. We can ask God to show us mightier things concerning our destinies, ministries, and even spiritual gifts. We can ask God to show us about Himself! He will do it.

God is not man or human. No question is stupid in His eyes. Remember God looks at the intent of the heart. A sincere and pure question presented to God will be accepted and responded to. What God has been teaching me for over a year now is that all I need to do is to ask. So confidently ask God what you do not know or understand.

PRAYING THE WORD OF GOD

†

Through studying the topic of prayer, training, and personal experience, I have discovered the Word of God to be so powerful and effective in prayer. The reason for this is that the Word of God not only conveys the opposite of the concern one is praying about, but praying the Word of God also translates to praying from a position of victory, a higher place, and also praying the will of God about the issue.

Praying the Word of God causes us to take our focus from the problem and bring it to the solution, which is the mighty power of God. By praying the Word, we release God's Word back to Him. God Himself swears by His Word to perform. *"The Lord said to me, 'You have seen correctly, for I am watching to see that my word is fulfilled'"* (Jeremiah 1:12 NKJV).

God also affirms that His Word will not return to Him void. His Word must perform what it was sent to do. *"For as the rain comes down, and the snow from heaven, and do not return there, but water the earth, and make it bring forth and bud, that it may give seed to the sower and bread to the eater, so shall My word be that goes forth from My mouth; It shall not return to Me void, but it shall accomplish what I please, and it shall prosper in the thing for which I sent it"* (Isaiah 55:10-11 NKJV). From these Scriptures God assures that He will do what His Word says about the situation we present to Him, according to the promise specific to that situation. If by the stripes of Jesus, we were healed, then we receive healing based on this Word. If there is no more condemnation to those who are in Christ Jesus, then we are guilt free in Christ Jesus. What and who God says we are, is exactly who we are! Forever in heaven, God's Word is settled (Psalms 119:89-90 NKJV). If God's Word is already established in heaven, then His Word must be established on earth as it is in heaven.

So, this is also why we approach God's throne boldly, because we can be assured of God's acceptance, not denial. When we ask in His name, He provides. Because God has spoken, He will always provide. He may not respond in the way we want, but He is definitely going to provide a solution. Faith is stirred up within and among us when we use God's Word in prayer. In turn, God responds mightily to faith. Collaboratively, faith, Word, the power of the Holy Spirit produces greater works-exploits!

The other reason why we should apply the Word of God in prayer is because the will of God is the Word of God. Praying the Word of God causes us to pray the will of God concerning the situation. Recall the Lord's Prayer, which prays: *"your will be done on earth as it is in heaven."* Let's say you need protection. Then, an example of praying God's will through the Word of God would include this prayer: *"Lord I thank you, because you have sent your Angels to take charge over me"* (Psalm 91:11 NKJV). "I take refuge under your wings. Lord my protection is in You. Thank you Jesus!"

The other powerful aspect of praying the Word of God is its creative ability when combined with the person of the Holy Spirit. This creativity of the Holy Spirit was first noticed in Genesis. Before creation, the Holy Spirit hovered over the earth. When God spoke; this is His Word, the Holy Spirit took hold of that Word, and brought things to being. God said *"let there be"* and it was (Genesis 1:1-3 NKJV). Subsequently, when we pray the Word such as, *"Oh Lord you are my strength,"* our strength is activated by the Holy Spirit, and we are empowered once again. *"In God we live and move and have our being"* (Acts 17:28 NKJV). Praying the Word of God in collaboration with the Holy Spirit produces creatively great results. That is why in God we receive exceedingly, abundantly about all we ask or need. *"Now to Him who is able to do exceedingly abundantly above all that we ask or think, according to the power that works in us, to Him be glory in the church by Christ Jesus to all generations, forever and ever. Amen"* (Ephesians 3:20 NKJV).

The Word of God permeates and disseminates every difficult situation. The Word of God is Jesus Himself. The Word became flesh and made his dwelling among us. We have seen his glory, the glory of the one and only Son, who came from the Father, full of grace and truth (John 1:14). Nothing is impossible with God. The Word of God can penetrate the hardest issues whether it mind body or soul. Here is the power of the Word of God: *"For the word of God is living and powerful, and sharper than any two-edged sword, piercing even to the division of soul and spirit, and of joints and marrow, and is a discerner of the thoughts and intents of the heart"* (Hebrews 4:12 NKJV).

Finally, praying the Word of God is a matter of faith. However, faith comes by hearing and by hearing the Word of God (Romans 10:17 NKJV). The only way to pray the Word of God is by hearing the Word, and that is achieved by intentionally reading and studying the Word of God. Purchase a Bible written in a translation that you can easily understand, such as NKJV, NLT or NIV. Set times to read the Bible and be able supplement that with listening to Bible Apps, if you can. As practice, I normally read the Bible, then listen to the same scripture while driving or while in the gym. Doing this helps reinforce the Word, and most of the time it brings clarity and different meaning or revelation. Meditate on the Word of the Lord day and night *"for they are life unto those that find them and medicine to all their flesh"* (Proverbs 4:22 NKJV). Study the Bible continually. *"Meditate on it day and night so you will be sure to obey everything written in it. Only then will you prosper and succeed in all you do"* (Joshua 1:8 NKJV).

ASK THE HOLY SPIRIT TO LEAD YOUR PRAYER

†

The most important gift that Christ left us was the gift of the Holy Spirit. No believer should ever confess the excuse of not knowing how to pray or do anything because Christ did not leave us helpless. In fact, Jesus Christ said that He was leaving for heaven but promised to give us a Helper who would guide us in all things! This Helper is the Holy Spirit, and He helps and guides us in all truth. *"But when he, the Spirit of truth, comes, he will guide you into all the truth. He will not speak on his own; he will speak only what he hears, and he will tell you what is yet to come"* (John 16:13 NKJV).

The reason for asking the Holy Spirit to help us in prayer is because frankly, as humans, we may not really know how to pray. When stuck with what to say, how to pray, and what to do before prayer, ask the Holy Spirit to help your prayer. This asking is not that "deep" or complicated either. Just say, *"Holy Spirit, help me to pray about the issue."* For example, at the start of prayer, I normally say: *"Holy Spirit I'm inviting you to pray,"* or *"Holy Spirit we are praying about (Name the issue)."* Then, say *"I submit to you, take over this prayer."* From there, I loosen up and let the Holy Spirit pray.

Every prayer should be directed by the Holy Spirit. Why is this? God is the discerner of minds and hearts through the Holy Spirit. Submitting to the Holy Spirit allows that which we cannot see in the heart, mind, and all around us to be petitioned by the Holy Spirit. The Holy Spirit intercedes for us with groaning. *"Likewise, the Spirit also helps in our weaknesses. For we do not know what we should pray for as we ought, but the Spirit Himself makes intercession for us with groaning which cannot be uttered"* (Romans 8:26 NKJV). The groaning are the inner things that we cannot tap to or do not know.

Collaboration with the Holy Spirit in prayer also allows for the deeper things of God to be revealed to us. The Holy Spirit is the Spirit and the mind of God, but this Holy Spirit also lives in each believer. This means the same Holy Spirit in you also connects to the heart and mind of God. Therefore, the Holy Spirit is able to share and release the mysteries and treasures of God to us. When this happens, the Holy Spirit prays the will of God regarding you concerning the issue. The Spirit reveals more. We tap into the inner courts, the Holies of Holies in prayer by the Spirit of God. Prayer is among the ways God uses to reveal His secrets and treasures to us. *"Call to Me, and I will answer you, and show you great and mighty things, which you do not know"* (Jeremiah 33.3 NKJV).

Oh, how I could emphasize the importance of allowing the Holy Spirit to pray with us. It is a partnership. Since He is the Spirit of truth, we cannot pray amiss or wrongly because the Holy Spirit will only pray the truth, and the right thing concerning the issue. Not forgetting that God sees the end from the beginning. *"I make known the end from the beginning, from ancient times, what is still to come. I say, My purpose will stand, and I will do all that I please"* (Isaiah 46:10 NKJV). He is the Alpha and Omega. Because God sees the unseen, what we cannot see, how much more critical is it to have His Spirit pray to align or avert what we cannot see and align all to God's purposes and destinies in prayer?

Allowing the Holy Spirit to take charge of the prayer leads to supernatural and mighty experiences with God. From experience, this is also where many impartations, visitations, deliverances, healings, prophesies, and other various gifts of the Holy Spirit occur.

Allow the Holy Spirit to pray with you by praying in the Holy Spirit or in tongues, as it is commonly known. Most of the time I start prayers by praying in tongues. Praying in tongues is also crucial when I am tired or have no words to tell God, especially when the issue is too weighty to pray in the natural language or understanding. Whenever I venture into praying in tongues I am normally amazed at the power of the Holy Spirit. If I had started prayer while tired, at the end, my strength is renewed. If overwhelmed, I experience deliverance at the end of the prayer. This leaves me feeling lighter with the weight being lifted off.

From personal experience, there are times the entire prayer will be in tongues and various tongues and the Holy Spirit then ends the prayer. Most of time the Holy Spirit prayer ends in worship and adoration to God. It's an out of sphere environment, praying from and in a different realm. When the Spirit takes over prayer, you cannot time Him. He can pray for two minutes or over two hours. The key is to be flexible, set aside ample time in pray, and let the Holy Spirit have His way in prayer. A good book to read to learn more about praying longer in tongues is called *Tongues Beyond the Upper Room* by Kenneth E. Haggin. Pray more in the Holy Spirit and let the Holy Spirit lead your prayer.

OUTCOMES AND BENEFITS OF PRAYER

†

There is more that prayers do besides providing answers and meeting needs. Holy Spirit steered and directed prayer does the following, but not necessarily in this order. Also, these are just few reasons for prayer that I am highlighting, but please know that there are many more benefits of prayer not listed here.

Enhances Spiritual growth

Since prayer is a mode of communicating with God, our relationship with Him gets developed and enhanced as we stay in communication with Him. Just like we would get to know a human being better the more we talk to them, so it is with God. As God reveals Himself to you in prayer, He also exposes some things in you. These may include what to do, what to let go, what to improve on, and the next steps. All these enhance spiritual growth.

Increases intimacy and fellowship with God.

When we grow closer to God in prayer, He also grows closer to us. *"Draw near to God, and he will draw near to you. Cleanse your hands, you sinners; and purify your hearts, you double minded"* (James 4:8 NKJV). *"The LORD is near to all who call on Him, to all who call on Him in truth"* (Psalms 145:18 NKJV). The more we spend time with Him in prayer, meditation, and in His presence, the more we get to know God's ways and God's heart. Prayer is one of the ways to get intimate with God. Here is where God reveals His secrets to you. From experience, intimacy with God may also manifest like a deep hunger for God to a desire always to be in His presence. In this stage, prayer and intimacy with God becomes a lifestyle. Prayer also becomes effortless, powerful, and effective.

Deliverance and Revelation

From personal experience, God really does a lot whenever we seek Him in prayer. Since prayers enhance our relationship with Him, God is spirit, truth, and holy. Therefore, He cleanses and removes anything that defiles Him from His presence. He does this through revelation and deliverance. For example, God may show you what you need to repent of, denounce or get rid of. He may reveal a hindrance in your life. As you pray, you will experience deliverance from what God has exposed, or what you have repented of. This happens privately in your prayer time with God. This happened to me through a process. It was as though I was going through a purging or cleansing, being purified while being pulled closer to God's presence. This aspect of deliverance does not negate any other deliverance that may be conducted for one in a gathering or church by ministers or pastors. So far I am learning that frequently God does things quite differently, and He supplements what He does in private in corporate environments.

Gifts and Impartations

God also imparts various gifts during prayer. Prayer activates the move of God and the move of the Holy Spirit. Although gifts and impartations are generally attained through the laying on of hands by spiritual leaders, at times God will impart to you directly during prayer. So approach prayer knowing that God can do whatever He wants during that time. Just be alert to know what is going on and be flexible and obedient to go with the flow of what the Holy Spirit is doing. Do not try to divert what God is imparting in prayer. If you choose to divert the move of God, you may have to experience that all over again, or you may totally miss Him.

You may ask then, "How would you know that an impartation or gifting occurred?" From personal experience, it is an inner knowing that is normally marked by doing or operating on a different spiritual level or through a gift that did not exist prior to that particular day or time in prayer. In my case, these always take me by surprise because I only notice the change much later in the midst of ministering or the next time in prayer. At times though, I will know immediately that something new was birthed.

So just stay in tune with the Holy Spirit. He will also confirm these new gifts and impartations. Lessons learned so far is that once surrendered and submitted to the Holy Spirit in prayer, surrender also to His directives and what He will do with and in prayer. Stay flexible in prayer and let the Holy Spirit have His way.

Prophesies and Declarations

God speaks to us directly when we pray. The way He speaks to each of us varies, but He responds to our prayers. To some, He may use an audible voice, and to others He may speak through dreams, visions, and trances. Still to others He may communicate through the mind or an inner knowing and to others through prophesies and declarations. The Holy Spirit is the God communicate through. Learn to know the distinct voice of the Holy Spirit or the way He communicates to you.

Whatever God prophesies or declares, He confirms. Frequently God may prophesy or declare somethings over you in private prayer, just to be confirmed later in a gathering of believers, through music, radio, or on a TV station. Whatever God communicates, aligns with His Word and His divine purpose for you. The Holy Spirit may show you something during prayer that is later confirmed when you read the Bible or through a teaching of Scriptures by a pastor or other believers. God may also communicate through His Angels and through fellow believers and spiritual leaders. At times God may prophesy or declare everything He intended to show you in prayer. However; God may also show you a glimpse or metaphor which can later be elaborated on or clarified by other believers or spiritual leaders who are gifted in the interpretation of dreams or visions. I encourage you to keep a journal of all encounters. I will discuss the reason for keeping a journal in the upcoming chapters.

Clarity of the Mind,
Sensitivity of the spirit,
Desensitization of the flesh

I write this section from personal experience. Uniquely, something happens internally when we pray. The mind, heart, and body become transformed during prayer. It is as though the Holy Spirit unclogs these areas of our lives. I have experienced this since 11th grade in high school. I normally preceded prayer time at dawn by reading the Bible. Once I would start praying out afterwards, I sensed my mind to be very clear and in tune with the heavens. Praying in this state of mind then makes prayer effortless and helps transitions in prayer to occur smoothly. With time, God cleanses the subconscious also. You may experience meaningful dreams, trances, and visions.

Praying also births an increased sensitivity to the Holy Spirit. This happens because God is a spirit being and we can only relate to Him though the Spirit. Prayer is one of the means that our relationship morphs into a heart-to-heart relationship where spirit, our human spirit, connects to God's Spirit. Because of this, we become in tune and sensitive to the presence of God, the voice of the Holy Spirit, and even other ungodly spirits in any given environment. We experience an increase in discernment, revelation, and other gifts of the Holy Spirit.

Because prayer keeps us connected to God through the Holy Spirit, the flesh becomes desensitized as we are being transformed from one glory to another. God is spirit, so as we utilize His Word to pray, as we submit to the Holy God to lead the prayer, we experience an inward and outward transformation. From experience, you may feel a sudden dislike of things that did not please God. For instance, you may stop listening to some type of music, reading certain books, or watching certain types of movies. Your social activities and circle of friends may change, relinquishing what did not please God to focusing on what is pleasing to God. You may also notice that leaving the past comes with such ease and without remorse. It is as though you have lost taste or interest in those things or persons. You will know that God is at working when you realize you no longer struggle with letting go than before.

Peace, Joy, and Rest

The other beautiful outcome of prayer is peace and rest. I call it "coming to a place of rest." Praying brings us to a place of peace and rest while still alive because in prayer we cast all anxieties, fears, and needs to God, and we know that God hears and will answer us.

We experience peace and rest in prayer through the Blood of the Lamb that has redeemed us and gives us the right to approach God in prayer without fear of retribution. When we utilize God's Word in prayer, we are actually proclaiming His promises for us. With assured promises we have peace because God Who promises is sure perform what He said He would do.

We experience rest through prayer as we declare God's Kingdom over our lives. When we pray, "Your Kingdom Come," as indicated in the Lord's Prayer (Luke 11:1-4), we are actually declaring the definition of that Kingdom on us. The Kingdom of God is righteousness, peace, and joy in the Holy Spirit. Prayer should and will be birthed by: a) righteousness—the Blood makes as holy as we relate to a holy God who we can only approach and worship in truth and Spirit; and b) peace—when we cast all to God He gives us the peace that surpasses human understanding. Prayer also guards our minds as started in the previous section resulting into peace according to Philippians 4: 6-7 which reads, "that says *do not be anxious about anything, but in every situation, by prayer and petition, with thanksgiving, present your requests to God. And the peace of God, which transcends all understanding, will guard your hearts and your minds in Christ Jesus.*" (NKJV)

Lastly, releasing God's Kingdom through prayer results in joy—the joy of the Holy Spirit. This is my personal testimony of experiencing this joy suddenly on my way to work one morning in 2014. I got to an intersection and realized that God had delivered me from depression and oppression. I had a sudden burst of joy and increased hunger for praise and worship music. This worship music remains the key music that I have preference for. With joy also came an increased gift or desire to dance. Oh, I love to dance for the Lord! I can dance subconsciously, in my brain, while driving. I love to dance to the Lord. Jokingly, I always share that I invented dance! The truth is that the dance moves themselves shocked me until one day while dancing in church a dear sister told me, *"Pauline I admire when you dance, you dance in the Spirit, and it is a heavenly dance that is why I always look at you while you dance."* I affirm that observation because I sense most of the time that the dancing is Spirit filled. I have always thought that Angels are there dancing with me. So, I dance for my redemption, for deliverance, for protection, for preservation, for salvation, for healing, for restitution, for recompense, and for strength. I dance in the joy of the Lord.

PRAYING FROM A VICTORIOUS POSITION IN SPIRITUAL WARFARE

†

Spiritual warfare is a vast topic that covers multiple areas. Prayer is one of the tools used in dealing with spiritual warfare, but it is not the only tool. Ephesians 6: 10-18 lists the entire armor of spiritual warfare, citing prayer as part of the armor in verse 18. So, if you were taught that prayer is the only way to combat spiritual warfare, then you were misguided. Underlined in these scriptures are the tools for spiritual warfare:

> *Finally, my brethren, be strong in the Lord and in the power of His might. Put on the whole armor of God that you may be able to stand against the wiles of the devil. For we do not wrestle against flesh and blood, but against principalities, against powers, against the rulers of the darkness of this age, against spiritual hosts of wickedness in the heavenly places. Therefore, take up the whole armor of God that you may be able to withstand in the evil day, and having done all, to stand. Stand therefore, having girded <u>your waist with truth</u>, having put on the <u>breastplate of righteousness,</u> and having shod your feet with the preparation of the gospel of <u>peace;</u> above all, taking the <u>shield of faith</u> with which you will be able to quench all the fiery darts of the wicked one. And take the <u>helmet of salvation,</u> and the <u>sword of the Spirit,</u> which is the <u>word of God; praying</u> always with all <u>prayer and supplication in the Spirit,</u> being <u>watchful to this end with all perseverance and supplication for all the saints;</u>* (Ephesians 6:10-18 NKJV).

In addition to the armor in Ephesians 6, spiritual warfare also involves dying to the flesh, walking in the Spirit, bearing the fruits of the Spirit, walking in holiness, maintaining our bodies as temples of the Lord, walking in humility and submission, being flexible to be chastened continually and refined by God, and allowing Him to transform us from one glory to another. Spiritual warfare involves perpetual bearing of weapons of righteousness on our right hand and on our left hand: *"By purity, by knowledge, by longsuffering, by kindness, by the Holy Spirit, by sincere love, by the word of truth, by the power of God, by the armor of righteousness on the right hand and on the left"* (2 Corinthians 6:6-7 NKJV).

Getting back to the main focus of the topic, which is prayer in spiritual warfare, let us start by defining spiritual warfare. Through salvation in Jesus Christ we are reborn in the spirit, by the Holy Spirit. Though we physically are human beings, on the inside we are reborn spiritually to the image of God. Christ lives in us by His Spirit. Given our new nature, we no longer or should no longer carry ourselves or engage in warfare from the flesh or the natural human nature but rather walk in the Spirit because we are now in the Spirit.

Because we are spiritual in nature, we operate also in a spiritual realm. That is why Paul cautions in Ephesians 6 that *"we do not wrestle against flesh and blood, but against principalities, against powers, against the rulers of the darkness of this age, against spiritual hosts of wickedness in the heavenly places. (NKJV)"* Spiritual warfare is engaging against these forces from a spiritual perspective. This is the simplest definition I can provide you.

The advantage we have is that we have been transformed into the image of God and Christ the King, and Lord of Lords is in us and we exercise His authority against these. With Christ in us, we approach spiritual warfare from a position of victory. With a predisposition of victory, all we have to do is cast out and decree for all that entails God's Kingdom to be established. "Thy Kingdom come, thy will be done on earth as it is in heaven." The victory that we have is established by overcoming, by the word of our testimony, and by the Blood of the lamb. The following Scriptures affirm the victory we have in Christ Jesus:

- *Colossians 1:15-18:* *"Jesus Christ created all things including the powers and principalities"* As the Maker, Christ has power over what He made, meaning Jesus Christ has power over satan and his cohorts. With Christ in us, we have the same power. He is the image of the invisible God, the firstborn over all creation. For *"by Him all things were created that are in heaven and that are on earth, visible and invisible, whether thrones or dominions or principalities or powers. All things were created through Him and for Him. And He is before all things, and in Him all things consist. And He is the head of the body, the church, who is the beginning, the firstborn from the dead, that in all things He may have the preeminence."* *(NKJV)*

- *Colossians 2:15:* Jesus Christ destroyed all the powers of satan, granting us the power. *"Having disarmed principalities and powers, He made a public spectacle of them, triumphing over them in it."* *(NKJV)*

- *Matthew 28:18-20:* All power has been given to Christ. *"Then Jesus came to them and said, 'All authority in heaven and on earth has been given to me. Therefore, go and make disciples of all nations, baptizing them in the name of the Father and of the Son and of the Holy Spirit, and teaching them to obey everything I have commanded you. And surely I am with you always, to the very end of the age."* *(NKJV)*

- *Colossians 1: 13-14:* We have been delivered from the power of sin and death. Satan comes to steal, kill, and destroy, but Christ gives us live. *"He has delivered us from the power of darkness and conveyed us into the kingdom of the Son of His love, in whom we have redemption through His blood the forgiveness of sins."* *(NKJV)*

- *Luke 10:17-20:* Christ in turn has given us the same power over Satan. *"Then the seventy-two returned with joy, saying, 'Lord, even the demons are subject to us in Your name.' And He said to them, 'I saw Satan fall like lightning from heaven. Behold, I give you the authority to trample on serpents and scorpions, and over all the power of the enemy, and nothing shall by any means hurt you. Nevertheless, do not rejoice in this, that the spirits are subject to you, but rather rejoice because your names are written in heaven." (NKJV)*

- *Mark 16:17-18:* We have the Name of Jesus to utilize as we exercise our authority in Him declaring and establishing God's Kingdom instead. *"And these signs shall follow them that believe; In my name shall they cast out devils; they shall speak with new tongues, they shall take up serpents; and if they drink any deadly thing, it shall not hurt them; they shall lay hands on the sick, and they shall recover." (NKJV)*

- *John 14:15-21:* We have a guaranteed Helper, the Holy Spirit; the Spirit of Power. *"If you love Me, keep My commandments. And I will pray the Father, and He will give you another Helper, that He may abide with you forever, the Spirit of truth, whom the world cannot receive, because it neither sees Him nor knows Him; but you know Him, for He dwells with you and will be in you. I will not leave you orphans; I will come to you." (NKJV)*

- *John 14: 12:* Christ left us a promise to answer us when we call on Him and do greater works. *"Most assuredly, I say to you, he who believes in Me, the works that I do he will do also; and greater works than these he will do, because I go to My Father. And whatever you ask in My name, that I will do, that the Father may be glorified in the Son. If you ask anything in My name, I will do it." (NKJV)*

- *Matthew 10: 7-8:* From this victorious position we can now establish heaven on earth. *"The kingdom of heaven is at hand. Heal the sick, cleanse the lepers, raise the dead, cast out devils: freely ye have received, freely give." (NKJV)*

There are more scriptures to add to this list that affirm our victorious position in mind. The key issue in spiritual warfare prayers is to make sure of our identity in Christ and appropriate the authority associated with that identify in collaboration with the Holy Spirit. Faithless religious practices become void. Once while visiting a church, its leader told me "In this church we do major spiritual warfare, no church in this area prays and fasts like we do." The sermon on that day was on generational curses. Later during prayer while in same church I was told I was too calm during prayer. In fact, the prayer leaders got upset with me. They said I needed to shake my hands, bend and twist, pace around, clap my hands violently, pray loudly and repeatedly say I plead the blood, I soak myself in the blood, saying this over and over, doing the physical actions in order to effectively engage in spiritual warfare. I could not do it, so I just thanked them and left.

As I left the church, the Holy Spirit reminded me that Christ became a curse for us. *"Christ has redeemed us from the curse of the law, having become a curse for us for it is written. Cursed is everyone who hangs on a tree"* (Galatians 3:13-NKJV). With that I prayed in bold faith:

> *Father in the Name of Jesus, I thank you that you have saved me and that Christ lives in my body. My body and everything that concerns me and are sanctified and holy. Lord I thank you because you have also sanctified by siblings, Mom, nephews and nieces because our household is saved. Therefore, because you became a curse for us, I rebuke every curse in my family from my father's side and mother's side in the name of Jesus. I lose myself and my family from every curse. I declare this curse (named the specific issue) broken. I release the Blood of Jesus that speaks greater things to speak and replace every curse spoken over my life and over our family. Lord your Word declares that You desire that I prosper in all things. I now declare prosperity, fruitfulness, multiplication, overflow and longevity in*

> *this area (named the specific issue) in the Matchless Name of Jesus. Amen!*

I experienced deliverance right away after saying that prayer. It was as though a weight was lifted off me. Since then, I've just been praising God and thanking God. Praying from a position of victory does not mean ignoring the negative issue. I am a realistic and very practical. I accept the negative issue exists, but I do not ignore it. Do not focus on the devil, witches, or principalities. You empower whom you focus on. In prayer and afterwards, do not dwell on it. Decree the Word of God, the promise associated with it. Establish the Kingdom of God in your situation. Believe in God. Believe in you, the greater power in you. Exert that Greater power in you, Christ in you in the person of the Holy Spirit, the Spirt of power. Doing that is combating spiritual warfare prayer from a victorious position!

HOW TO PRAY WHILE WAITING
FOR THE ANSWER

†

Among the greatest frustrations and challenges for believers is the waiting period between the initial prayer and the time the answer to that prayer comes. Normally, this is a period of both spiritual and emotional testing as to whether we can persevere in trusting God for what He promised or what we asked Him for. This waiting period is a test of faith. As shared earlier, the prayer of faith is what matters because when we pray, we are believing God for what we prayed for. Below are tips on what to do in the waiting period. Most of these are from personal experience and what the Holy Spirit as taught me so far.

I strongly encourage you to press on in prayer until you receive breakthrough to the issue you have petitioned God. The prayer at this point shifts from petitioning to the prayer of expectation. Just like as a pregnant mother anticipates a child after nine gestational months, so are we required to continue with expectant perseverance as we wait for the answer. Hannah's story in 1 Samuel encourages me in the waiting period. In this story Hannah continued to pray until she received her answer.

> *This went on year after year. Whenever Hannah went up to the house of the Lord, her rival provoked her till she wept and would not eat. Her husband Elkanah would say to her, "Hannah, why are you weeping? Why don't you eat? Why are you downhearted? Don't I mean more to you than ten sons?" Once when they had finished eating and drinking in Shiloh, Hannah stood up. Now Eli the priest was sitting on his chair by the doorpost of the Lord's house. In her deep anguish, Hannah prayed to the Lord, weeping bitterly. And she made a vow, saying,*

"Lord Almighty, if you will only look on your servant's misery and remember me, and not forget your servant but give her a son, then I will give him to the Lord for all the days of his life, and no razor will ever be used on his head." As she kept on praying to the Lord, Eli observed her mouth. Hannah was praying in her heart, and her lips were moving but her voice was not heard. Eli thought she was drunk and said to her, "How long are you going to stay drunk? Put away your wine." "Not so, my Lord," Hannah replied, "I am a woman who is deeply troubled. I have not been drinking wine or beer; I was pouring out my soul to the Lord. Do not take your servant for a wicked woman; I have been praying here out of my great anguish and grief." Eli answered, "Go in peace, and may the God of Israel grant you what you have asked of him. "She said, "May your servant find favor in your eyes." Then she went her way and ate something, and her face was no longer downcast. Early the next morning they arose and worshiped before the Lord and then went back to their home at Ramah. Elkanah made love to his wife Hannah, and the Lord remembered her. So in the course of time Hannah became pregnant and gave birth to a son. She named him Samuel, saying, "Because I asked the Lord for him" (1 Samuel 1:7-20 NKJV).

The Prayer of Faith is what moves God. The Bible repeatedly warns in of unbelief. In fact, unbelief is sin because it devalues God's power. In Romans, Paul gives the history the Israelites and warns present believers to watch out, lest they miss heaven because of unbelief. Paul reminds us that some Israelites died in the desert because of unbelief missing the Promised Land. Subsequently, believers can also miss their promises because of unbelief. *"But with whom was he grieved forty years? Was it not with them that had sinned, whose carcasses fell in the wilderness? And to whom swore he that they should not enter into his rest, but to them that believed not? So we see that they could not enter in because of unbelief"* (Hebrews 3:17-19 NKJV). So while we wait for an answer, we should wait in faith, trusting that God whom we prayed to, trusting His promises that He will bring forth answer. *"Let us labor therefore to enter into that rest, lest any man fall after the same example of unbelief"* (Hebrews 4:11 NKJV). This is now walking by faith. *"The just must live by faith"* (Romans 1:17 NKJV).

This faith walk in prayer is also what we apply in order to hold on to the unshakable promises of God. While waiting for the answer, we must hold on to the Word. If God says He heals, healing must manifest. If He says He will provide for you, just as He provides for the birds of the fields and the micro-creatures in the deep oceans, we must believe that provision will manifest. We pray then stand on the promises of God; His unshakable Word and watch God fulfill His promises to us.

Thanksgiving and praise are other powerful tools to use while waiting for an answer. Personally, I have experienced much, and at times immediate breakthrough whenever I have reverted to thanksgiving and prayer. At times when I start thinking about the issue, the Holy Spirit will sing an affirming song in my heart. I have learned to sing along as the Spirit sings in my heart. I open my mouth and join the Holy Spirit in singing. Normally I pay attention to the words of the songs. It's amazing how God communicates back. Oh, I have countless occasions where the Holy Spirit has birthed new songs or just started singing when my mind was pondering on an issue! The songs or words usually assure me of what God is doing. This usually brings me to "a place of rest".

Thanksgiving and praise are not limited to songs though. Entering God's courts with thanksgiving and praise can be done through prayer as well. Most of the time when reminded of an issue I have already petitioned to God; I frequently start like this: *"Father I thank you for this day. I thank you that I lack no good thing. I thank you for watching over your Word to perform me. I praise you in advance that this book is a bestseller. I glorify you for what you are doing right now concerning this issue. I praise you for an overwhelming answer! I thank you for the overflow an exceedingly much more that will accompany this answer. I bless you. I honor you."* Each time I pray this way I have received a fresh surge of power, assurance, and renewed faith.

The other aspect of living while waiting on God is living a lifestyle that does not compromise the promise we stood on in prayer. This requires personal determination and intentional living taking the stance that no matter what happens, we will do the opposite of God's Word in order to get an answer. Attaining this level translates to unshakable faith. This what the Apostle Paul refers to when he talks about the "weapons of righteousness on our right hand and our left hand." Staying faithful to the course despite the delay to the answer. This also means no short cuts, no manipulation, and no lying to get the answer. No resorting to alternative means to get answers, including settling for the second best or other options. These weapons of righteousness on both hands, means taking a firm stance. It is a different aspect of spiritual warfare where we stand our position through our character and interaction with all people on a daily basis. Below is what Apostle Paul said in 2 Corinthians 6:3-10:

> *We live in such a way that no one will stumble because of us, and no one will find fault with our ministry. In everything we do, we show that we are true ministers of God. We patiently endure troubles and hardships and calamities of every kind. We have been beaten, been put in prison, faced angry mobs, worked to exhaustion, endured sleepless nights, and gone without food. We prove ourselves by our purity, our understanding, our patience, our kindness, by the Holy Spirit within us and by our sincere love. We faithfully preach the truth. God's power is working in us. We use the weapons of*

*righteousness in the right hand for attack and the left
hand for defense. We serve God whether people honor us
or despise us, whether they slander us or praise us. We
are honest, but they call us impostors. We are ignored,
even though we are well known. We live close to death,
but we are still alive. We have been beaten, but we have
not been killed. Our hearts ache, but we always have joy.
We are poor, but we give spiritual riches to others. We
own nothing, and yet we have everything. (NLT)*

Although the above scriptures are geared towards ministry,
they also apply to all of us in our daily lifestyle, including
our lifestyle after we have prayed.

On compromising, from the same chapter, Apostle Paul
warns:

*Don't team up with those who are unbelievers. How
can righteousness be a partner with wickedness? How
can light live with darkness? What harmony can there
be between Christ and the devil? How can a believer
be a partner with an unbeliever? And what union can
there be between God's temple and idols? For we are
the temple of the living God. As God said: "I will live
in them and walk among them. I will be their God, and
they will be my people. Therefore, come out from among
unbelievers, and separate yourselves from them, says
the Lord m don't touch their filthy things, and I will
welcome you. And I will be your Father, and you will
be my sons and daughters, says the Lord Almighty"* (2
Corinthians 6: 14-17 NLT).

Additionally, I caution against seeking ungodly alternatives,
short-term solutions to a problem, or quick fixes. These
do not defraud us of God's perfect will for us, causing us
to settle, making us permissive, but they also make us
susceptible to counterfeit open doors for demonic operations.
Short cuts, quick fixes, and alternative second bests do not

please God; they fade quickly. *"Wealth gained hastily will dwindle, but whoever gathers little by little will increase it"* (Proverbs 13:11 NET). The wealth in this scripture is not limited to just money; it means provision you may want. Anytime we seek alternative to ways to meet our needs and exclude God, we fail to acknowledge our God as the source of our provision. Such actions do not please God.

A good story that warns us against seeking alternative means is the story of King Asa, who died when he did not seek God to treat him. *"The events of Asa's reign, from beginning to end, are written in the book of the kings of Judah and Israel. In the thirty-ninth year of his reign Asa was afflicted with a disease in his feet. Though his disease was severe, even in his illness he did not seek help from the Lord, but only from the physicians. Then in the forty-first year of his reign Asa died and rested with his ancestors"* (2 Chronicles 16:11-13 NLT). It is highly likely that if King Asa would have turned to God with prayer and repented, he may have lived and reigned longer. God is merciful, kind, and loving. He says that if we repent, he hears and heals. *"If my people, who are called by my name, will humble themselves and pray and seek my face and turn from their wicked ways, then I will hear from heaven, and I will forgive their sin and will heal their land"* (2 Chronicles 7:14 NKJV).

Romans 5:1-4 sums up the reason for the testing and waiting to period to this when it says, *"Therefore, having been justified by faith, we have peace with God through our Lord Jesus Christ, through whom also we have access by faith into this grace in which we stand, and rejoice in hope of the glory of God. And not only that, but we also glory in tribulations, knowing that tribulation produces perseverance; and perseverance, character; and character, hope. Now hope does not disappoint, because the love of God has been poured out in our hearts by the Holy Spirit who was given to us."* (NKJV)

Normally, our minds are affected during the period between prayer and waiting for the answer. I wrote a blog that I posted on Facebook in the spring 2016 that ministered to me greatly. In it, I emphasized the importance of keeping our minds steadfast in hope and in the promises of God. I shared some strategies on how to counterattack unbelief by simply switching your mind set to God. The title of the blog was "Flip It." As we conclude this chapter, I will present the entry from my blog and trust that it will help you:

> More and more, I'm beginning to understand the role of attitude and mindset in spiritual warfare. It requires a decisive personal stance on how to address unexpected day-to-day issues. We need to be prepared at all times, not letting our lamps run out of oil. We must be filled with the Spirit as we're vigilant and alert, ready at all times, because we never know what will happen next. In short, we should be ready for the unexpected with a mindset that disputes life's challenges with the authority we have as believers.
>
> When faced with sudden emergencies, bad news, anxiety, fear and the general uncertainties of life, our first reaction must be to turn the negative into a positive by declaring the Word of God and taking productive steps to remedy the situation. "Flipping it" is, in itself, a type of spiritual warfare that dictates our thoughts, emotions, reactions and actions.
>
> Kings Hezekiah and David are perfect examples of believers who flipped the negative situations they unexpectedly faced. Let us mirror what they did.
>
> *FLIP IT by turning to prayer.* This is what the Lord says: *"Put your house in order, because you are going to die; you will not recover"* (2 Kings 20:1-6 NKJV). When King Hezekiah was told he would

die from an illness, he flipped the bad news by refusing to accept it and turning to God. Hezekiah turned his face to the wall and prayed to the Lord, *"Remember, Lord, how I have walked before you faithfully and with wholehearted devotion and have done what is good in your eyes." (NKJV)* And Hezekiah wept bitterly. Then the word of the Lord came to Isaiah: *"Go and tell Hezekiah, 'this is what the Lord, the God of your father David, says: I have heard your prayer and seen your tears; I will add fifteen years to your life'"* (Isaiah 38:1-5 NKJV).

Earlier on, King Hezekiah had been threatened by another nation that blasphemed God and sought to wage war. Hezekiah approached the Lord in prayer, and the Lord sent His own angel to fight the Assyrians, restoring Hezekiah's kingdom. Hezekiah received the letter from the messengers and read it. Then, he went up to the temple of the Lord and spread it out before the Lord. And Hezekiah prayed to the Lord (2 Kings 19). Again, Hezekiah flipped his situation by praying.

FLIP IT by encouraging yourself in the Lord. "Why so downcast oh my soul. Put your hope in God!" (Psalm 42:5 NKJV). This may well have been the song David was singing after the attack at Ziklag. Though weary and emotionally drained, he strengthened himself in the Lord. David was greatly distressed because the men were talking of stoning him: *"Each one was bitter in spirit because of his sons and daughters. But David found strength in the Lord his God"* (1 Samuel 30:6 NKJV).

Distraught, David had no confidant, and yet people were looking to him for guidance. He had no one else to turn to but God. He flipped it by encouraging himself in the Lord. You, too, may be experiencing your own battle—waiting, enduring, on the verge of a life-draining situation. Funga ukanda (Swahili for "fasten your belt"), gird up your loins, shake off the dust, gear up, stand up. Greater is He who is in you. Look up to the mountain that is the Lord, and ask him to strengthen you.

FLIP IT by confessing God's promises and word. "The Word of God is Life and is also alive" (John 1:1). God's Word always contradicts every negative issue. Where you cannot, the Word can; where sickness is, the Word brings healing; where bondage holds us back, the Word brings deliverance, where sin is, the Word brings forgiveness through the blood of Jesus and through mercy and grace. Where impossibilities reign, the Word brings all possibilities.

Romans 10:10 offers a compelling reminder of the power of confessing God's Word. It's not only in the knowing, but in the constant meditation on His promises: "For with the heart one believes unto righteousness, and with the mouth confession is made unto salvation." (NKJV)

God's Word, our daily bread, is what brings us salvation. There's nothing impossible in the eyes of the Lord. "For the word of God is living and powerful, and sharper than any two-edged sword, piercing even to the division of soul and spirit, and of joints and marrow, and is a discerner of the thoughts and intents of the heart" (Hebrews 4:12 NKJV). Profess God's Word to flip every negative situation

God's Word always contradicts every negative issue. Where you cannot, the Word can; where sickness is, the Word brings healing; where bondage holds us back, the Word brings deliverance, where sin is, the Word brings forgiveness through the blood of Jesus and through mercy and grace. Where impossibilities reign, the Word brings all possibilities.

FLIP IT by trusting in the Lord. There's a big difference between confessing God's Word and actually trusting that it will be activated and creatively bring about a solution. *"Trust in the Lord with all your heart and lean not on your own understanding. In all your ways acknowledge Him, and He will make straight yet paths"* (Proverbs 3:5-6 NKJV).

FLIP IT by shifting your trust from friends, resources, mentors and pastors to God. Turn to the Creator of all, not His creation. Trust through persistent faith. Even if that faith is but a mustard seed, it can still move mountains.

God is not a man, so he does not lie. *"God is not human, so he does not change his mind. Has he ever spoken and failed to act? Has he ever promised and not carried it through?"* (Numbers 23:19 NLT) Flip it by trusting in God completely.

FLIP IT by waiting on the Lord. There are multiple advantages to this. God is never late with His answers. God is timeless, so He always responds at the right time. God can bring to pass instantly what once seemed delayed.

Psalm 90:4 is a good reminder of God's sovereignty when it comes to timing: *"A thousand years in your sight are like a day that has just gone by, or like a watch in the night." (NKJV)*

This attribute is further reinforced in 2 Peter 3:8: *"Do not forget this one thing, dear friends: With the Lord, a day is like a thousand years, and a thousand years are like a day." (NLT).* We are also renewed as we wait on the Lord—spiritually developed and matured as we wait. *"He may be purging us and shaping us to be qualified, usable vessels"* (2 Peter 2:21 NKJV). *"They that wait upon the Lord, shall renew their strength"* (Isaiah 40:31 NKJV).

So wait on God, because His timing is always perfect. Wait in thanksgiving, worship, and praise. Wait as you continue pushing and pursuing, focusing on the Lord for the breakthrough. Wait while remaining consistent in whatever assignment or calling He has assigned you, avoiding distractions. We wait in the Spirit, not by our flesh. This continuous, expectant mindset is one that we must have. Flip it by waiting on the Lord.

FLIP IT by standing firm. This is the ultimate test of mind and will, requiring a determined stance with no looking back or wavering. According to the Apostle Paul: *"After you have done all, then stand. Therefore, put on the full armor of God, so that when the day of evil comes, you may be able to stand your ground, and after you have done everything, to stand. Stand firm then, with the belt of truth buckled around your waist, with the breastplate of righteousness in place, and with your feet fitted with the readiness that comes from the gospel of peace. In addition to all this, take up the shield of faith, with which you can extinguish all the flaming arrows of the evil one. Take the helmet of salvation and the sword of the Spirit, which is the word of God. And pray in the Spirit on all occasions with all kinds of prayers and requests. With this in mind, be alert and always keep on praying for all the Lord's people"* (Ephesians 6:13-18 NKJV).

Now that you have the full armor of God, flip it by standing on the Unshakable Rock who is greater in you than any situation you're facing. Flip it while knowing that the Right Hand of the Lord is doing valiant work on your behalf.

This week, flip it in prayer, flip it by encouraging yourself, flip it as you speak the Words of Life— His words, His promises. When you confess, salvation comes.

Flip it as you put all of our trust in the Lord. Flip it as you wait in thanksgiving and praise. Finally, flip it by standing, staying tied and being hooked on Christ, the solid rock. It's not by your own might or power that you can change the unexpected, but by His Spirit; read Zechariah 4:6.

Be encouraged. God is faithful and dependable.

HOW TO INCORPORATE PRAYER
INTO DAILY LIFE

†

Now that we have reviewed various aspects of prayer and how easy one can approach prayer, we can now incorporate prayer in our daily lives. If you have read up to this section of the book, I have highlighted the simplicity of prayer, where it does not necessarily require set activities, times, or routines to pray. Instead, we can pray wherever and whenever. Discussed in this chapter, I share some recommendations about how to engage actively in prayer on a regular basis.

First and foremost, it is important to make praying a priority because as believers, prayer is essential in communicating with God. Secondly, prayer is the language of the spiritual realm. Having been translated in Christ, prayer becomes our weapon for changing the spiritual realm whether we are influential in God's realm or principalities and powers of darkness. Prayer is one of the means of bringing God's Kingdom to earth.

Commit to making prayer a priority now that you gathered how to go about praying. Initially, I would advise that you identify set times for reading the Bible and praying. From experience, it is better that the time spent reading the Bible is used to know the Word of God. Then, you should proceed to praying. The reason for this is because the Word of God is the will of God, and therefore, we can apply the Word of God while praying in order to not pray amiss. Secondly, the Word of God is the promise of God. We affirm these promises in prayer, and they are released or manifested in our lives. *"This book of the Law shall not depart from your mouth, but you shall meditate in it day and night, that you may observe to do according to all that is written in it. For then you will make your way prosperous, and then you will have good success"* (Joshua 1:8 NKJV).

You can start with five minutes of reading a chapter of the Bible before prayer then praying for the duration of time the Holy Spirit will lead you. You should not get stressed over how long you pray. Whereas this is encouraged, do not go into prayer wandering how long you will last in it. As shared earlier, all prayer should be led of the Holy Spirit. As you develop in your prayer life, the Holy Spirit will help you along and increase you in prayer. We can start as humans, and a teacher or a prayer leader may coach and train you in prayer, but eventually if you submit to God, the Holy Spirit will increase your prayer. *"Blessed are those who hunger and thirst for righteousness, for they will be filled"* (Matthew 5:6 NKJV). If you ask God for more, He will give more to you.

To cultivate discipline in prayer, identify set times and a place that you can go to pray. This place or space should uninterrupted, giving you the ability to pray without being interrupted. If you are able to pray three times a day do so, but I recommend having a schedule of praying at least twice a day—at the beginning of your day and at the end of your day. Given changing work schedules, you can define the start and end of your day, especially for those who work during the night or another alternative schedules.

Outside the set times for prayer, praying can be done while driving with eyes open, over lunch, or while completing house chores or running errands. Remember that prayer does not necessarily have to be audible. You can pray while standing in que at the post office. You can silently pray, even with tongues while in a crowd, you can pray while taking walk! The point here is to not to limit or "box" prayer to have to be done in a particular way. With this kind of flexibility, you now realize that you can prayer whenever and wherever!

Next you may question whether the length of prayer is crucial. My response to that is to lean on the Holy Spirit and let Him direct the prayer. It is the prayer of faith that matters anyway. Do not worry much about how long, but just be flexible with the Holy Spirit and allow His free flow.

Based on personal experience, the length of prayer varies. I have prayed for two minutes and received breakthrough, yet in some prayers I have tarried. My experience with God though is that He tends to share or show me more after I have tarried longer. Although, at times He has also lifted me to higher realms of His presence, shortly after starting praying. I encourage you though to practice tarrying longer in prayer and doing so by praying in tongues.

When you spend time with the Holy Spirit in prayer, He will tell you when He wants to say or show you something. I would describe it as an inner knowing. At times you may sense a change in your surrounding or it could be a change to the tone of your voice while praying or a stillness. I must warn though that once here with the Holy Spirit, you have no control. He is the one in charge. It is best to have Him have His way. Do not rush to cut short the Holy Spirit when He in acting during prayer or anywhere else. Doing so cuts you short instead, and you miss out on what He intended to do. So, learn to allow the Holy Spirit to have a free flow during prayer or in other areas of your life.

Once you have set time, always have a journal with you in your prayer area. The journal is critical to write what God shows or tells you. Once written down, you can always reference and pray over what God has shown you. I have to appreciate referencing the journal because what God shares always affirms and encourages me in this walk. The journal also serves as a ledger to write and track prayer requests and answers to those prayers. These would in turn be your ledger of your testimonies, where you chronicle the testimonies of the Lord; what God has answered or responded to. We overcome by the Blood of the Lamb and by our testimonies. Halleluiah!

NOW PRAY. TALK TO GOD IN THE
LANGUAGE YOU UNDERSTAND

†

This book was birthed out of a deeper desire and hunger for each believer to recognize the power of prayer that they can institute and walk in independently. It was also created to help believers realize that each person can access and hear God through prayer. The ability to pray and hear God independently will avert dependence on other people to "hear God for you" or seek God on one's behalf. This is the freedom and liberty we have in Christ—the freedom to relate to God with confidence that whatever we ask in His Name, He will hear us!

When believers have the confidence to pray and receive from God, they will avoid deception from false teachers and fraudsters who scam and exploit many financially, emotionally, and physically under the disguise of "I am praying for you." Being independent in prayer also curbs idolatry by not constantly contacting someone first to pray for you, or worse yet, being totally dependent on a "prayer line" without developing a prayerful life. A respected minister once shared that there are many believers who assign others their prayer lists while the believer him or herself does not take any initiative to pray for him or herself.

We are now in the spring of 2016 when this book is being written. Unfortunately, we are also in an era of rampart false ministers in church. How sure are you that whomever you sent money to or a so-called "personal prophet" or "my prophet," "mentor," "spiritual leader," or even "prayer partner" is praying for you? As saints who have been given free access to God by the Blood of the Lamb we now have the ever-present help of the Holy Spirit who assists us in prayer. It is my prayer and hope that this book provides some guidance and builds and steers you to pray independently.

So take courage and step out in prayer. Talk to God in the language you understand. Given that Jesus already gave us an outline for prayer and we have been set free from religious mindsets and practices, let us approach God boldly in prayer. God wants to do more with us in these last days. It's now 2016, we are living in the times of "greater and mightier works" that Jesus promised in John 14:12: *"Very truly I tell you, whoever believes in me will do the works I have been doing, and they will do even greater things than these, because I am going to the Father." (NKJV)*

We are living in the season of the greater outpour of the Holy Spirit as promised in Acts 2:17-21:

> *And it shall come to pass in the last days, says God, that I will pour out of My Spirit on all flesh; your sons and your daughters shall prophesy, your young men shall see visions, your old men shall dream dreams and on My menservants and on My maidservants. I will pour out My Spirit in those days; and they shall prophesy. I will show wonders in heaven above and signs in the earth beneath: Blood and fire and vapor of smoke. The sun shall be turned into darkness, and the moon into blood, before the coming of the great and awesome day of the Lord. And it shall come to pass. That whoever calls on the name of the Lord shall be delivered. (NKJV)*

We are in the times where God wants to show us the secret things, to see the unseen and hear the unheard! Oh Church, we are living in the times of the outpour of the Spirit of God—the Spirit of Fire, the wind of the Spirit! God is moving in our season. Let us grasp God to His fullness. Open your mouth, talk to God. Get to know Him. Allow

Him to minister to you. Take your stance, move boldly, and talk to God the best way you know how. God is waiting for you. He is about to blow your socks off as you develop this powerful relationship with Him through prayer.

PRAYER AND ACTION GO HAND IN HAND

†

The entire Christian walk is all about faith. Whether we read the Word of God, sing praises, fast, or pray, all must be done in faith. However, the Bible teaches that faith without works is dead. Whereas the goal of this book is to free you to pray independently, after praying we need to act of what we have prayed for.

> But someone will say, "You have faith, and I have works." Show me your faith without your works, and I will show you my faith by my] works. You believe that there is one God. You do well. Even the demons believe—and tremble! But do you want to know, O foolish man, that faith without works is dead? Was not Abraham our father justified by works when he offered Isaac his son on the altar? Do you see that faith was working together with his works, and by works faith was made perfect? And the Scripture was fulfilled which says, "Abraham believed God, and it was accounted to him for righteousness." And he was called the friend of God. You see then that a man is justified by works, and not by faith only. Likewise, was not Rahab the harlot also justified by works when she received the messengers and sent them out another way? For as the body without the spirit is dead (James 2:14-26 NKJV).

It would be unwise to pray fervently about an issue without taking steps towards that issue. This is so important, especially if you were raised up in doctrines that taught that believers should spend hours in prayer and go on long periods of fasts in order to get breakthrough. Yes, prayer and fasting are critical, but we should not make them mere practices without taking steps towards what one is praying for. Prayer and action go hand in hand. This is what it means to have

Faith and Works working simultaneously together towards the desired outcome. First the prayer must be conducted in faith and must align to the will of God, not of personal selfish gain. Second the prayer must be led of the Holy Spirit. With the Holy Spirit leading prayer, this same Holy Spirit will direct you on what you need to do—the action associated with that prayer.

Consider the following examples of how prayer, faith, and action went hand in hand. In numerous accounts of King David's reign, David frequently sought the Lord before venturing to war for direction. This seeking was his prayers. Whenever God responded, David took action and pursued his enemies. David did not just pray and stay still, he still acted. Joshua was another example of action. In order for the walls of Jericho to fall, Joshua, the Priest, the worshippers and the army of seven marched around the wall (Joshua 6). Initially there was prayer, followed by action. As I am writing this I am even intrigued by the lineup of this match. First were the priests and the army. To me, this translates to prayer in form of thanksgiving and worship, an army, God's presence, which was the Ark of the Covenant followed by another army.

As believers, we are watchmen, prayerful people over our cities, territories, families, children, marriages, and careers. As intercessors we must stand on guard while at the same time take action. King David was such a man. He had been in secret prayers while in the caves as a shepherd. He had already experienced and seen God's saving and delivering power. I believe that most of David's intimate revelations occurred in the hills and valleys while he was a shepherd. So, when it came time for Goliath, David took action.

I applaud setting apart times to seek God in prayers and fastings, but it is crucial that we are not caught up in the religious spirit of "works," always praying and not taking action. Without faith we cannot please God; Hebrews 11:6

(NKJV), *"And faith without works is useless."* (James 2:20 NKJV), *"Hence prayer without action is pointless!"* So if you have prayed for a job, fill out the application, study the employer, prepare for the interview, dress appropriately for the interview, and show up for the interview! Leave the rest to God. If you prayed for business opportunities, write your business plan, conduct a market analysis, seek the Holy Spirit to lead to mentors and advisors (Proverbs 15:22 and Proverbs 11:14 NKJV). Review your budget and develop a strategic financial plan, especially if you plan on leaving a fulltime job to start your business. Review legal and insurance requirements. You want to be well informed before you venture in. Collectively, these are actions of faith from the prayer concerning a business.

Like everything else in our walk with God, there is a part that we must actively play. Even Adam was granted the earth at creation but he had to take care of it. Prayer is not only communication with God, but it is partnership with God. God's purposes must be accomplished through us by the help of the Holy Spirit. As you pray, ask God to show you the steps you should take. Be encouraged, God is faithful and dependable. He watches over His Word to perform it. After you have acted on those steps, offer God prayers of praise, worship and thanksgiving as you wait on God for the answers of the prayers and watch what God will do!

EMBRACE LOVE, EMBRACE GOD'S GOODNESS, EMBRACE JOY

†

I would like to conclude this book with a personal testimony of God's visitation during a time of prayer in early September 2016. I shared this testimony in one of the blogs that I regular post in social media. I titled this testimony "A Prayer of Thanksgiving."

Jeremiah 31:3: *"I have loved you with an everlasting love and I have drawn you with my loving kindness."* (NKJV)I woke for morning devotion as usual, but the moment I hit the prayer mat, I was overwhelmed by a strong presence of God's love, God's joy, and God's goodness. The air or the presence was thick yet transparent. I could touch it, and I could feel it.

The moment I touched the air I heard the Lord say, *"Embrace My love. Embrace My joy. Embrace My goodness. Pursue Me out of love."* By this time, I was so overwhelmed that I switched the prayer to a prayer of thanksgiving. As I meditated on these throughout the day I realized that God has already given us love, joy, goodness, favor, health, wealth, everything. All we will need to do now is embrace, accept, and walk in that which we have already been given.

So this week instead of asking God for this and that; consider switching your prayers to:

- ◆ Lord I embrace Your joy and thank You for Your joy.
- ◆ Lord I accept Your love and thank You for Your peace.
- ◆ Lord I receive Your loving kindness and thank You for new mercies every day.
- ◆ Lord I walk in Your protection and thank You for shielding me and for the angels assigned to me and my household.

- ◆ Lord I receive Your salvation, deliverance, and healing and thank You for freedom.
- ◆ Lord I embrace Your provision and thank You that I lack no good thing.
- ◆ Lord I embrace Your Presence and thank You for the fullness of joy in Jesus Name.

This week, embrace God's love, goodness, kindness, mercies and joy. Embrace, accept, and walk in them. You are in God's presence. Amen!

SUPPORT WITH PRAYER

†

Pauline is available to teach about prayer
and lead prayer in small or large settings.
Contact information is listed below

Pauline Adongo
The Ministry of Jesus Christ International Inc.
P.O Box 2572
West Chester, PA 19380
Email:padongomjc@gmail.com
Website: www.paulineadongo.com
Facebook, Instragram,Youtube and Twitter

CALL TO SALVATION & FILLING
OF THE HOLY SPIRIT

†

Scripture(s) John 14:6-7: "Jesus *said to him, 'I am the way, the truth, and the life. No one comes to the Father except through Me. If you had known Me, you would have known My Father also; and from now on you know Him and have seen Him.'(NKJV)* Also, 1 John 1:8-9: *"If we say that we have no sin, we deceive ourselves, and the truth is not in us. If we confess our sins, God is faithful and just to forgive us our sins and to cleanse us from all unrighteousness." (NKJV)*

Maybe you are at your wits end and you just want God to reach out to you and realign you to the marvelous plan He has for you. Invite Him to come in and take the lead by saying this prayer:

> Dear God, I come to you. I accept your Son Jesus Christ as my Lord and Savior. I believe that Jesus died and rose again for my sins that I may receive salvation. I therefore repent of my sins and ask for your forgiveness. I renounce sin. Lord Jesus now come to my life both in me and in everything that concerns me. Come in Lord Jesus and be Lord over my life and align me to the path and plan you have set for me. In the name of Jesus Christ, I pray. Amen.

Now invite the Holy Spirit who will serve as your helper and guide among many things in this new life. Say the following:

> Holy Spirit, I now welcome you to reside me and take over every aspect of my life. I submit to you Holy Spirit; guide me in knowledge, wisdom, revelation, and discernment and counsel to walk and accomplish the plan God has for me. Holy Ghost, fill me with your gifts that I may

experience the fullness of God in this new life, in the name of Jesus I pray. Amen! Oh beloved of the Lord, the Holy Spirit now resides in and with you. Watch out for what He is about to do!

With arms opened wide, welcome to the Kingdom of God! The next step is to look for a local church whose beliefs and doctrine align with the Word of God. I have already prayed that the Holy Spirit will connect you with the right believers who will help and guide you to maturity in Christ Jesus. On your end, set some time at least twice a day to pray and read the Bible. Prayer is simply talking to God. Ask the Holy Spirit to teach you how to pray, and then just pray. To start, pray when you first wake up and talk to God the way you talk to a friend you respected and be open to God, telling Him everything. If you can only pray 5 minutes twice a day, do that, then increase your prayer time daily. With time the Holy Spirit will mature your prayer life if you stay consistent.

You may read the Bible before or after your prayer time. Purchase a version or download a Bible app that you can easily understand such as the New Living Translation (NLT) or New International Version (NIV). I prefer the New King James Version, but occasionally, I read other versions when I need clarification. When you are about to open the Bible, ask the Holy Spirit to illuminate and bring clarity to what you are about to read. The Holy Spirit is very good at this. This is His job—our helper. He reveals the truth to us. Start by reading the book of Proverbs and the Gospel of John. You can read one chapter of Proverbs when you wake up and a chapter from John before bedtime. Purpose to memorize a scripture a day and meditate on the scripture that caught your attention. With time, the Word of God will become alive in your heart and in your thoughts. Before you know it, you would have read the entire Bible. When you get there start anew. By the help of the Holy Spirit this is how we grow; it takes personal responsibility.

OTHER BOOKS BY THE AUTHOR

†

THE ALTERNATIVE PLAN - Released in the summer of 2015, this book was written for young professionals in the work place as well as young adults from high school to those just launching into their first careers, to assure you that God can still realign your life to fit the plan He intended for you. This book was written to those questioning their future, and it ministers to the wounded and those seeking security in their lives. This book highlights the lies Satan uses to sabotage the plan of God for you. It demonstrates God's ability to clean up and restore to fullness, even the greatest mess. Through reading this book, may you receive salvation, healing, deliverance, restoration, and restitution in the Name of Jesus through His Blood! The purpose of this book is to bring hope to the reader and provide direction on how to get back to the plan God intended for you.

ISBN-978-0-9898247-6-7. Hardcover. 55 pages

Each of us was born with gifts and talents. Some still struggle with identifying their gifts, others struggle with how to develop those gifts. In this book, you will detect possible clues that are linked to your gifts and how they manifest. Throughout the book, you, will be shown how to identify and develop your gifts and talents; in partnership with the Holy Spirit and with man (God appointed mentors). This book is for EVERY believer because all believers are ministers. This book is for those contemplating ministries but who have no clue what to do; for Ministers in Training or ministry interns, for ANY church worker; for deacons, elders, ministers and pastors. It is a foundational manual: 101 in ministry, but the Spirit inspired words in this book can be applied IN ALL vocational areas including church and the workforce. Be equipped, the harvest is plenteous!

ISBN-978-1-5127-2760-9. Hardcover. 104 pages

Titles and talents are NOT prerequisites for service. Each believer is uniquely and individually gifted by God and has the capacity and capability to minister to others. Jesus Christ in His mandate to the His followers said "go ye"; there are no special titles or designations tied to this mandate other that "those who believe" (Mark 16:14-20). The main objective of this book is to encourage each believer to recognize the platform God has given them to accomplish the Great Commission. This platform may be a career, vocation, business, home environment or department in a church. This platform is what I refer to as "your pulpit". Each believer has one. Once you have recognized your pulpit, I discuss how both natural gifts, talents and spiritual gifts can be applied collectively to minister to others. The harvest is still plenteous. Having been already empowered by Jesus, let us join together in gathering the harvest. Go ahead and minister wherever you are!

ISBN-978-1-3127-4316-6. Hardcover.55 pages

Books can be purchased from
www.paulineadongo.com

Printed in the United States
By Bookmasters